Mindful Habits for Better Parents

How to Stop Losing Your Sh*t and Start Owning Parenthood

Aileen Jarvis & Rowan Roffe

contained within this document, including, but not limited to, errors, omissions, or inaccuracies.

Table of Contents

Mindful Parenting Made Simple

A FREE GIFT TO OUR READERS

As a way of saying thank you for your purchase, we're offering our readers special access to the ultimate mindful parenting checklist.

This checklist includes:

- 3 Mindful techniques to turn conflicts into closeness.
- 11 Powerful phrases for positive parenting that you can use <u>TODAY.</u>
- 15 Self-care strategies to help you own parenthood!

Visit this link: <u>https://tinyurl.com/mindfulchecklist</u>

Introduction

"Children are educated by what the grown-up is and not by his talk."

-by Carl Jung

Remember the time when the little one was coming into the world, gracing you with their presence while breaking nearly all the bones in your body? Or at least it felt like that. Remember the moment the doctor told you that you finally did it and that the worst was now over?

Fast forward three years and you are sitting on the kitchen floor scraping up Nutella or Vaseline that your toddler decided to paint the floor and walls with? And as soon as you take them to the bathroom to wash off the chocolate spread from their hair, you discover that your little one has draped the toilet seat and bathroom floors with toilet papers.

It is hard to process any sane thoughts at the moment. You are so angry that you are about to lose your sh*t. How in the world did the doctor so conveniently lied to your face telling you that the worst was over? And here you are, barely remembering the last time you take a break from cleaning the house or the last time you get a full 8 hours of sleep.

Sometimes you wish you believed other parents when they told you that YOU REALLY HAVE NO IDEA ABOUT HAVING KDIS UNTIL YOU HAVE KIDS! Children not only make you occasionally want to lose your sh*t, but you are also cleaning up after their sh*t, literally and figuratively. Seeing my children aspiring to be Pablo Picasso with Nutella and Vaseline, it's hard to remember the excitement I felt when they came to the world. I was ecstatic when they started crawling and even more thrilled when they took their first steps. But, had I anticipated what that meant, I would have probably appreciated some more time and perhaps more warnings of what children are capable of.

Dear readers, we are completely with you and quite frankly have been in the same boat as you. Parenting is hard. It feels like the whole world is conspiring against you. The man upstairs is watching from above, enjoying the back and forth running you do to get your child to eat or stay still while you are changing their leaking diaper. It feels like everyone else is sitting on a greener grass, having a glass of wine; meanwhile, you have been sent up onto the stage to perform a comedy gig - and you don't even know any jokes.

Being a parent is the world's toughest job. You are on call 24/7. You get no overtime, no PTO, and no definite job description. You are expected to deal with all source of problems, and losing your mind isn't one of the solutions.

So, what are we suggesting? Not to get frustrated when your kids misbehave right under your nose and keep doing it, just to get you all riled up? Or not to react when they are getting on your nerves demanding for some candy they don't remember the name of but saw it in the department store?

It is very easy to lose control of the situation and yourself in such frustrating moments and, like you, we have shared similar experiences at some point in our parenthood. Here's one thing we learned: those frustrating moments were the moments when staying calm and composed saves you your time and energy later in life.

When kids are young and naïve, they are all set to explore things on their own. They want to feel like kings and emperors who ruled the world and the people in it. Just with a motion of their hands, they got whatever they wanted. They want to feel the same control, freedom, and sovereignty. And we all know how the stories go. Whenever they felt challenged or scared, they brought out the big guns and the catapults… Kids; they may not have real weapons, but they do have the ability to make endless demand, cry, and cause a power struggle. Their tantrums and mischievousness may be a great story to share one day at a family gathering, but what about right now? How can we deal with their tantrums and mischievousness?

That is the big question that this book will answer. How can we, as parents, keep our sanity and be understanding? How can we be seen as empathic while maintaining boundaries and rules? How can we demand respect while being perceived as supportive and friendly and not dictatorial? How we can navigate through power struggles using practical behavioral adjustment strategies that don't come off as deliberate and pushy. How can we establish good habits for better emotional awareness and meaningful interactions?

This book will steer clear of any assertive tips but rather focus on mindfulness techniques for both parents and the kids, especially for first-time parents. We shall start this mindfulness journey with you, of course, and then move onto implementing similar techniques and methods on your kids. Together, we shall kick this off with a basic understanding of the daily struggles of parenthood, the frustrations and then introduce you to the many definitions of mindfulness, how to practice it and what crucial role it plays to improve the parent-child relationship.

This book isn't exactly scholarly, but it does hold some great insights and scientific research studies to help you understand the mental and cognitive processes better.

Why should you listen to what we have to say? What makes us the experts at parenting? Well, it is only fair to introduce us first so that, throughout the book, you know who we are and where we are coming from.

We are Aileen Jarvis & Rowan Roffe. We have come together to write this one of a kind book while both working as child development specialists. Our work takes us through the daily struggles that parents face as their children grow up. Inspired by the way in which we see children and their unique tendencies, and how it can affect a parent, we decided to write this parenting book that gives a voice to the frustration, so many of you parents feel. Parents of two and three children, respectively, we have incorporated both our own professional knowledge and personal experience in the writing of this book. We hope you will enjoy reading it through and find the answers you came looking for.

Chapter 1: What's Up, Chuck?

Parenthood is tough, and it usually takes the highest toll on the mothers, especially the ones who are mothers for the first time. They are figuring out the many changes in their bodies. Some may be dealing with postpartum depression without actually knowing that they have it while taking care of a newborn who is completely dependent on them for everything, forcing them to put their own needs second to that of their child's.

We get it. It's difficult. We have been through similar situations. Our stories echo the same battle and worries. We share your exhaustion and frustration… This is why Rowan and I are motivated to make parenthood easier for ourselves and for other parents to be. The feelings of worry, frustration, and anger during parenthood is normal, but these feelings shouldn't be normalized if we want to achieve a more rewarding parenting experience.

Remember we are not managing inconvenience. We are raising a human being. Hence, we need to support each other and learn the habits that can make parenting a little easier. After all, most of us know there is more to come after the terrible twos.

Enter toddlerhood and adolescence.

The age where your lovingly-festooned house no longer looks like one. The age where everything turns chaotic with a lot of running involved but rarely having anything accomplished. The age where there are endless tantrums in a day and only more to come to the next. The age where quietness signals the calm before the storm and likely a sign of something sneaky going on behind your back. Maybe we are drawing a picture too dramatic. Still, even if nothing of the sort goes on into your house with a toddler, it is natural for you to feel parental frustration at some point. The annoyance can result from the kid not listening to you or obeying you. It can also result from misbehavior and ill-manners of your children, exacerbated by your struggles at work. Whatever the cause of your irritation is, it is an understandable response to the stress of parenthood even though it shouldn't be. Why do we say it shouldn't be? It is because the majority of the time, this frustration, even though difficult, is manageable. If you cannot control your response, your emotional outburst can result in an unintended effect, setting a less-than-stellar example for our kids.

Whenever we come across parents complaining to us about the use of foul language, the first thing we ask them is about the environment in their homes. Is it conducive to the kid's development? Does the way the parent discipline the child involve yelling and verbal and emotional mistreatment? Is the kid exposed to continuous fights between the adults in their life? Is one or both parents short-tempered? All of these questions allow us to better understand a child's experience and what's going on inside the mind of the kid. You see, kids are like sponges. They socialize by absorbing and imitating whatever they see and listen. They are quick to pick things up as their brain is constantly evolving. Therefore, it is crucial that children are exposed to the environment that is conducive to their development and that we parents exhibit the type of characters we want them to take after.

So how can you deal with the everyday frustrations that come with being a parent? How do you handle your emotions without causing a scene in front of your kids or punishing them when they might be mirroring you?

In this first chapter, we are going to be looking at this in detail and talk about how we can better understand the role we play in nurturing strong-willed, compassionate and emotionally intelligent kids.

To do so, let's first understand what frustration is or looks like so that we feel more prepared to deal with it later.

To end the first habit of frustration, you must start with noticing when you are frustrated and seeing if the cause is internal or external. This is the first key habit in adopting the first stage of mindful parenting

Introduce the habit of noticing when you are frustrated and analyzing the cause of it. Let's start there.

Understanding Frustration

Frustration, in psychology, is considered a natural but emotional response to opposition. It usually comes in the form of annoyance, anger, and disappointment. Frustration breeds from resistance to fulfilment of a person's goal or will and likelier to intensify when that goal or will is blocked or denied. In simpler terms, it is the uncontrollable rage that we feel when we find that something hasn't gone the way we expected it to. Parental frustration is similar. It is an expression of anger often accompanied by irritation and disappointment, resulting from unmet expectations.

There are two forms of frustration – internal and external. Internal frustration is the result of unmet personal goals, expectations, instinctual drives, needs, and desires. It can also be due to perceived deficiencies such as low self-esteem, lack of self-discipline, or other fears. Another cause of internal frustration can stem from internal conflict when one personal goal interferes with the other and causes one to feel conflicted and less sense of control. It can also lead to cognitive dissonance. If we were to see an example of internal frustration in our daily life, it looks something like this: you are having a difficult time at work. Responding to the workload, you spend more time at the office, which makes you miss precious time with your kid. However, because you are a parent, your child is the reason why you aren't able to give your work the time it deserves so that you can be a step closer to your professional goals. When you are at work, you think about your kid, and when you are with your kid, you think about work. You are bound to feel conflicted having to balance between work and kid and perhaps feel guilty that you sometimes have to choose work over your child.

On the other hands, external causes of frustration encompass conditions that aren't in our control and our need to control the uncontrollable leads us to feel like a failure. These causes may include physical roadblocks where other people and things get in the way of our goals. We may also feel frustrated due to our perception of wasting time. An example of frustration from external causes might look something like this: you are at the office and waiting for some report from another colleague to look at before you go home. You are already getting calls from your spouse because it is getting late, and you don't want to be stuck in the traffic for another hour before going home to your family. But that report is nowhere to be seen, and you have just been told that it will take another hour or so before the colleague finishes it. This situation is due to someone else's poor working ethic and is out of your control. You can't do anything to drastically change the outcome, so you feel frustrated as you have no control over the situation.

Parental Frustration and Its Primary Causes

Parental frustration usually arises from feelings of insecurity and uncertainty, which is a by-product of our inabilities to fulfil our or our kid's needs. When the needs are hindered by some external stimuli, frustration occurs. It can also originate when these needs are unsatisfied or constantly ignored. We feel agitated, angry, depressed, aggressive, or annoyed, and sometimes, we take it out in the worst form –violence. Violence isn't always physical. It can also be emotional, mental, or verbal.

Parental frustration is inevitable. When you are raising a kid, frustration is a given. They may be quick learners, but sometimes, they test your patience with making you repeat things over and over again. You want them to grow up to be the best version of themselves, and in doing so, you invest your time, energy, and money. Getting frustrated is normal. But how you deal with that frustration is the big question! Before we get to answering that, how about we take a look at some of the most frequent reasons that lead to parental frustrations? These reasons are the most common ones we come across when working with various families. We bet that the frustration you feel is also due to one of these reasons.

Undisciplined kid/kids

Kids who don't listen or purposely misbehave are the #1 reason for parents becoming frustrated. Not only is it embarrassing for the parents to deal with the misbehavior when it happens in crowded public spaces, but it also makes it harder for parents to apply positive discipline. Positive discipline is hard to accomplish when dealing with misbehavior because children respond more quickly to punishments, and positive disciplining requires more effort from parents. The literal meaning of the word discipline isn't punishment, but rather "to teach." This means that to discipline, we have to be mindful and use tools like communication and empathy to change a child's behavior rather than trying to stop their behavior by inflicting emotional or even physical pain with punishment. Sometimes, when we see other kids behaving well, it makes us even more frustrated because we know we are giving our all to foster our kids in the best way. We are always trying our best to meet their needs, listening to them, showing patience around them, and whatnot. Yet, they still choose to misbehave and throw tantrums. This makes parents wonder where are they falling short and what needs to be done.

Little Sense of Accomplishment

Raise your hands if you can relate to this: how many times have you felt that no matter how much you do for your kids, you always fall short at some point? There is always something lacking that makes you doubt your capabilities and feel like a failure. There are days when we feel like we didn't get anything done despite not having a minute to sit down and relax. This "little sense of accomplishment" can make us feel helpless when piling with an endless to-do list of laundry, grocery, etc. We feel like we have spent the day catering to the needs of just your child, and even then your child still doesn't want to go to bed calmly at the end of the day. This can lead to frustration when you think about all the things you have to do and worry about pushing them for the next day, which by the way, already has another to-do list.

Poor Character in Kids

We want our kids to grow up as well-mannered and obedient individuals. Kids who lack a sound and disciplined foundation often become the cause of frustration among parents. After all, they are often viewed as a reflection of us and our parenting capabilities, and we want them to have a good character. We want them to have all those qualities we aspire to and want to see in ourselves as well as them. We want them to speak with integrity, not use foul language, have self-confidence, and depict good manners. When our kids lie, talk back to us, use a poor choice of words when angry or agitated, these things make us feel like we didn't do well enough.

Disorganization in the House

Nobody likes a disorganized and cluttered space. We have all been injured with the Lego blocks lying on the floor. We have also fallen prey to cleaning up after our kids are done playing because they chose sleeping over cleaning when you asked them to pick one of the two. Although you got them to sleep, you were left with the cleaning and arrangement of their million toys; and don't even get us started on how it just takes them a mere second to pull them all out from the toy basket when they can't find that one tiny army action figure. You get it, right?

No one likes to come home all tired and then feel they have to pick up after everybody and cook and clean. Parents aren't machines. We get tired too. But our children are young and naïve. They don't get the concept of being tired. All of this clutter, even though expected in a house with young children, can unexpectedly deepen our frustration.

Sibling Quarrels

Having one child can already be a handful; however, having more than one can create another source of frustration. While developing their sense of ownership, siblings can turn into rivals. One child will want what the other is playing with, and the other would want what the other sibling is playing with. They are never content with what they have and don't know how to share. Then, after trying to get their way and failing to get away with it, they come to you crying and complaining about who hit whom first and so on. This can take a toll on a parent who loves both the kids. Somehow, you manage to get them calmed down and learn to share, but that peace treaty only lasts a few minutes, and they are back at fighting over a new toy.

Having a Full Plate

One of the major mistakes that many parents make is being over-committed. We feel like we have to do it all, and we have no time for ourselves. And the fact that we can't do it all and have to compromise our personal needs is just outright frustrating.

Dealing With the Anger and Irritation

Now that we have established the many reasons that can cause parents to feel frustrated and lose their calm, the next step is to figure out how to deal with it. Being a parent constantly comes with new challenges. Some days, we feel like everything will be alright and that we will learn to live with it. But some days are downright tough and drain every last bit of our energy and patience.

Days when the little one falls sick and constantly cries or days when they keep on whining over every little thing from their dress to the food. During those days, it is easy to lose sight of the bigger picture, which is raising them to be a good person, instilling in them good habits and values. But as stated earlier, mindful parenting and positive disciplining start with you. Therefore, if you are feeling frustrated over something, the first step to addressing this emotion is to be aware of it. Examine the cause of this emotion and focus on how you can positively respond to it.

Importance of Recognizing the Negative Feelings

Anger and irritation are usually the first indications that something is not going right. However, before letting them overwhelm us and make us lose our minds, we need to understand where it is stemming from. Generally, is this frustration due to some internal or external causes? What behavior from your child triggers it? Is it some repeated action like not eating their vegetables or resisting a bath?

You need to recognize those feelings of negativity and address them. The best way to do so is to accept them as they come. Accept that you are feeling angry and don't try to cover it up with some other emotion. Find an outlet for this emotion if you must. Secondly, please don't blame yourself or feel ashamed for feeling the negative emotion. It is okay to feel a little mad and agitated over how your kid makes you feel. What is not okay is acting negatively in response to these emotions. The best way to deal with frustration, especially the one with an external source is to recognize the wisdom of the Serenity Prayer—"God grant me the serenity to accept the things I cannot change; courage to change the things I can; and wisdom to know the difference."

We come across many parents who are extremely overwhelmed because they find their experience as parents different from their expectation. They keep bottling up their emotions, which drive them to a breaking point. Every emotion, be it negative or positive, needs addressing and acknowledgement. Acknowledging our emotions is necessary for emotional acceptance.

Many mothers, for instance, complain of unsupportive partners. Feeling unsupported and lack of teamwork creates negative feelings, which can be amplified when children misbehave. Sometimes children are just being children, and we adults lack the emotional intelligence to address our issues that we sometimes unconsciously projected them onto the kids. Hence, if at any time you feel frustrated and don't know how to react, here are a few things you can do to help yourself feel better and in a calmer state of mind.

One of the recommendations we make for parents when they feel that they are losing control of their emotions is to distance themselves from the thing that is triggering the anger or irritation. This means if your work, partner, or your kid is getting on your nerves and you sense an outburst of negative emotions ready to take over, temporarily remove yourself from that space so that you give yourself some room to breathe. Excuse yourself to avoid any conflicting situations, which can only make matters worse. Go into another room and let the emotions run through you or until the wave of emotions subsided. Don't go back into the situation unless you are more clam and have accepted the negative emotion. Take at least ten deep breath until your heartbeat slows down, and you feel more in control over your emotions.

If you have little to no control over the trigger, and there isn't much you can do, the best way to deal with the overwhelming feeling is either to talk to someone. Talking through your emotions with a close friend can be beneficial. You can also write them down in a journal. The idea is to not let your emotions get all bottled up because they are going to manifest themselves in some ways, and the way they manifest themselves might be in the manner you prefer. Once we have talked through our emotions or expressed them on a piece of paper, we will start to feel calm again. Most of the time, when we are overwhelmed, the best way to handle it is to get these feelings out of our systems. Talking through our feeling and writing them down is a great opportunity to reflect on the situation and start to see things more clearly. The biggest disadvantage of bottling up our negative feelings is that this can cloud our judgment and affect our sanity. We need to learn to express our emotions constructively so that our emotions don't emerge in a way that negatively impacts the people we care about.

Another effective but quite random advice we recommend to parent is to take the approach Fred Rogers adopt (for completely different reasons) in the popular TV show *Mister Rogers' Neighborhood*. Interestingly, changing clothes can also be a mood changer as it allows our mind to think about something other than the negative emotion. The idea is to get busy elsewhere so that one stops thinking about the frustration and let go of it. This is referred to as making a mental and physical shift from a negative emotion to a positive one. A simple act such as changing clothes can help let go of the emotions one feels too strongly. Once you are able to remove yourself from the situation temporarily, you will be able to see the situation more clearly, figure out why you felt so out of control, and learn to deal with it more positively next time.

Why Does Modern-day Parenting Look So Hard?

Since this question comes up quite often when we coach parents, it is only fair that we make a comparison between our generation and that of our parents. Think about it; they seemed to have done it so easily. They fed, cleaned, and looked after us. They had time to attend kiddie parties, wedding events, and other social parties without thinking a dozen times who will watch the kids and whether we should go at all or not. Of course, we are busier than our parents, but that only means more stress and frustration for us. With the amount of time we have with our kids, we have to teach them good manners, instil in them good habits, discipline them, and make them grow into responsible individuals.

We have worked with more mothers than you can imagine, and every time we are amazed at how smart, intellectual, well-resourced, and educated parents of today are. The parenting problems we faced today are so different from the issues faced by our parents decades ago. Issues like cyberbullying, data privacy, screen time, etc. are all the problems that emerge and become more prevalent in the last decade. The level of frustration many parents of today feel when dealing with these issues is astounding.

Frustration seems to be the threads that weave the modern-day parents together. But it isn't just frustration that is the problem. It is also self-doubt, worries, anxiety, and judgmental looks that we sometimes get from our parents and grandparents who might think we are doing a poor job of parenting. Sometimes we feel ashamed of the messiness and how chaotic our life is. Other times we feel like we don't have what it takes to keep up with others and thus feel guilty, which makes us even more frustrated.

So why do we feel this defeated, burned out, and inadequate all the time even though we are better resourced than any generation of mothers?

Let's take a look at the differences in modern-day parenting and old-style parenting and understand why it is harder to raise good kids today than it has ever been. (Just to be clear, this is a gross generalization of the modern and traditional parenting.)

Nowadays, our expectations as parents have risen. The bar for what is considered "good parents" are set higher. And the worst part: support has dropped. We have come a long way from an era where shaming, beating, scaring, and threatening children was considered a norm. Now, although it's a good thing in general that we are more aware of the life-long impact of such old practices, the shift in the child-rearing models has eliminated many important players that helped with raising a child. Think grandmas, aunts, cousins, and neighbours. In the old-time, many families used to have joint family systems that offered comfort and support. There were whole tribes taking care of children, supportive neighbourhoods where kids played outside in the sun all day, and family members who were always happy to take in the kids when we wanted some time of our own. Now, we have to worry about hiring someone professional, relying on their expertise, paying them. If that isn't an option, we have to pick and drop them at the daycare so that they can be looked after while we are at work.

Being a parent, especially a mother, is an all-consuming job. We feel constantly bombarded with what ideal parenting should look like and fear being judged or shamed for the way we parent. There is never-ending pressure of looking and acting a certain way, thanks to all the advertising and celebrity images that we see every day. They seem to have it all figured out and look flawless like they are able to sleep 8 hours a day and have time to do their hair and makeup. What many fail to remember is that we only see the best part of people on social media. Celebrities often have a full-time helper. We, on the other hand, are the ones cleaning their poop, changing their diapers, spending the whole day looking after them. Expecting our parenthood to be as effortless as what we see on social media is not realistic.

Another reason for the added pressure is that women of today aren't just expected to become full-time moms. We are also expected to build our careers simultaneously and be exceptional at work and at home. Then, we are also expected to look good, appearance-wise, not show any signs of ageing, discomfort, or pain even when the high heels are killing us, and the earrings are just too heavy. And once we are done showing off to the world how great we look and feel, we have to come home to our kids and worry about their cleaning, eating, food sensitivities, internet safety, sustainability, manners, school affairs, and their emotional and physical wellbeing. It seems like too much, doesn't it?

The abundance of knowledge and wisdom we receive from the digital world urges us to do more with that knowledge. However, conflicting ideas, ever-changing dynamics, and false bits of advice linked to promotional products and services make it harder for us discern which advice is essential and applies to us.

We are sleeping less, suffering from low energy levels, and have too much to worry about at once. The worst thing about parenting is that you never get any cheat days. Once a parent, always a parent! This role becomes your whole life, and that starts to get you.

We feel exhausted because we have to fill in so many roles at once. We have to be our kid's best pal, their playmate, mentor, teacher, nutritionist, maid, and their mother. Women, in particular, battle with exhaustion as they are wired to care about the needs of others and often put those needs above our own.

Moreover, we are also up against the biggest marketing giants. They are feeding our kids with senseless, gender-biased, addictive messages. They are normalizing the drinking of Coke, eating a Big Mac for lunch, heading to Hardy's for some milkshakes leaving us parents to deal with the corresponding urges and tantrums. Not to mention the excessive screen time and what it is doing to our kid's minds, eyesight and body is an issue big enough to write another book about. Imagine having to protect a little one from all that is out there for them and constantly feeling like you're losing the battle.

The challenges that come with modern parenting can be an exhaustive list; however, the goal of mindful parenting is for us to be present and aware of our external and internal situations so that we can respond thoughtfully to our children's behaviors and actions in a way that nurtures the relationship.

Chapter 2: Mindfulness Exposed

Have you ever had a day where you were already late to work, and as you walked towards the door, you felt something grab you by the feet? Like two little hands, clinging onto your skirt or pants, looking up to you with their puppy-dog eyes? As much as you would want to capture that moment in your memory forever, you know that if you don't make it past the door this very minute, you are going to be awfully late and miss the presentation you have been tirelessly working on for weeks.

The first thought that crosses your mind is, "Oh God, not today" because you are fully aware of what follows after the little one has gotten your attention and moved your heart with that gesture. Parenting can be extremely hard when kids keep testing your patience and challenging your ways. When Rowan and I started our career as a child development specialist, we were naïve back then. Even though we had studied child psychology in-depth and dealt with the pressures of it firsthand, we still lacked that balance we hoped to create. You know that level of calm and peace in the house where there is a strong parent-child relationship, and the kids don't misbehave. We always wanted that kind of peace in our house too. But with more than one kid in the house, that seemed like an impossible dream.

Like many other parents, we tried every trick in many parenting books to become better parents and establish an amazing relationship with our children. Still, nothing seemed to provide us with the result we wanted. Our children were immuned to the way we disciplined them. Their compliance was short-lived, and disobedience continued. They hated us when we tried to discipline them, and it was costing our relationship. That was the time when there was this crazy hype about mindfulness. Everyone was talking about it with enthusiasm. Articles were being written, papers being published, research being done. It seemed to be the next big thing that the world had waited for.

Reading about it and discussing its many benefits with ourselves, we wondered if we could try to apply some of the mindfulness practice at home with our kid. Initially, we were skeptical that something so vague would ever work, but the minute we started, we noticed little changes in the behavior of our kids; we knew that we were a step closer to the dream home environment we had wanted.

The kids started to become more expressive about their demands and needs, showed patience when told to wait, and began confiding with us the things that bothered them. Conversations about anything and everything become a common thing in the house, and together, as a unit, we all worked to meet each other's expectations. This might seem like quite a poetic explanation of what worked for us but, to tell you the truth, it was no light-bulb moment. We learned through trial and error, modified things our way, and actually made an effort to change the things we wanted to change.

Since we were new to the terminology, and there was little information about mindful parenting, we had to make some major changes in our attitudes and behaviors as well. Since we knew that implementing mindfulness practices in parenting meant we had to first walk the talk, learn to wear our kid's shoes and see the world from their eyes, it was extremely hard not to lose our tempers when dealing with them and then address every tantrum differently. This might seem quite a lot to take in for now, but by the time you are done reading this book, we are hopeful that you will feel comfortable practicing and honing these techniques.

In this chapter, let's first go through the basics of mindfulness, mindful parenting, and practices every new mindful parent can use to keep negative emotions in control. Once we have these sorted out, we'll move on to some role-playing and see how the kids view their parents and what goes in their minds. Yes, things are going to get super exciting moving forward.

What Is All the Hype About Mindfulness?

The best way to describe mindfulness is this: Imagine you are driving around the city, perhaps on a trip all by yourself. You arrive at the destination, and the people there ask you how the drive was. It is then that it clicks that you hardly remember anything about it. You remember passing through some fields, some big advertising boards, but not the route or specific turns you took. The whole drive was a blur.

Another example can be watching TV while eating dinner simultaneously. Some people have a hard time recalling what they had for dinner last night because they were operating on autopilot. Let me be clear, there is nothing wrong with enjoying food while watching our favorite TV shows; however, in a culture where productivity is valued, multitasking can be a slippery slope that leads to mindlessness—a state where one seems to lose track of time completely and is rarely able to recall anything meaningful regarding the occurrence. It is a state of being in the autopilot mode where our body repeats actions that we are used to performing without the brain ever registering them. Did you know that humans are in an "autopilot" mode 47% of the time (Killingsworth & Gilbert, 2010)?

How do we ever let our mind wander this way? It's like being in a dreamlike state without actually falling asleep. This is very similar to being drunk as the brain isn't capable of actively making wise decisions. Imagine you hit someone crossing the street while driving because you weren't paying attention to the new crosswalk in your neighborhood. This sounds scary, doesn't it? But, being on autopilot is human nature. In some ways, it helps the brain saves energy and helps us get through our everyday life. However, at times this mindlessness can work against us and our intentions.

For example, we sometimes fail to notice the signals our body gives us to rest or that there is an early symptom of more serious illnesses. Maybe our back is aching, and because it doesn't interfere with our daily activities, we ignore it and carry on with our lives until it becomes a more serious issue.

Mindlessness isn't just harmful to us, but can also later impact the lives of people around us. Being in an autopilot state helps prevent our brain from becoming overload. However, it may come at an emotional cost when it slips into the areas of our lives that require more forethought. When we sleepwalk into our choices, this increases the likelihood of us making poor choices causing us to be more stressed and anxious. The same research mentioned previously, for instance, also suggests that the more we let our minds wander, the less happy we are as we fail to notice the beauty of things around us.

Now imagine a state completely opposite of mindlessness. This is what we call mindfulness. It is coming out of the autopilot mode and taking control. Mindfulness is becoming aware of the present, aware of what we are doing and what we are not doing. It is the ability to be fully human so that we don't get swept away by our emotions. We all possess the quality to become mindful. We are born with it; however, kids have an easier time to be mindful. See how babies look at you with their eyes wide open even when they do not understand a word you are saying? Notice how they smile back at you when you grin at them? These are all the ways they are being mindful of their presence with yours. Sadly, due to the Western culture of productivity and multitasking, many children will lose their natural tendency to be present over time, unless we nurture this mindfulness in them.

Since we already possess mindfulness since birth, all we need to do is cultivate it using simple strategies so that we can appreciate the "now" and begin to accept things without judgment. These basic strategies include breathing techniques, sitting quietly with our self-reflective thoughts, enjoying peaceful walks, and mindful meditation. There are many benefits associated with these simple techniques, the majority of them leading to a complete sense of awareness which we want to foster in our kids.

Being fully present help to us to be emotionally grounded, allow us to shift from negative thinking to a more positive one, and enable us to make choices that best reflect our interests. It also helps us to be more aware, reduces stress, and enables us to approach things with more compassion, kindness, and less judgment.

Since you are role models for your kids, it is only fair that we start with you.

Mindfulness and Parenting: What's the Connection?

Paying attention has become so difficult these days. With the advent of phones and increased screen time in the form of media channels like Netflix, Amazon Prime, Disney, and Hulu, we are always looking for a more meaningful time. This screen usage upsurge has also affected our focus as we try to do more things but less focus to do them. So, we keep on multitasking, hoping to have a foot in everything and not miss out.

Even when we do try to fully engage in one thing, our mind is constantly wandering elsewhere, worrying about something entirely different. We are always geared at thinking about the next thing and how we are going to do that. In short, we have stopped living in the moment, or appreciate the here and now. When we're not mindful, a majority of our time is spent thinking about the past or the future—creating unnecessary emotional focus toward the things or events we have no control over. How many times have we stopped to wonder about the impact of our own mindlessness on our little ones? Do they deserve such a distracted parent?

Mindful parenting focuses on giving our kids the best thing in the world: our undivided attention and time. It is our presence, our acceptance, and an opportunity to create meaningful, strong, and long-lasting relationships that they want. And we all know how good it feels to be fully immersed into something that we love doing. We feel so alive and so empowered. We feel valued and on cloud nine. Imagine our kids feeling the same way. Imagine our children looking up to us with compassion in their eyes because they feel looked after, safe, and cared for. This is truly the best gift we can ever give them.

Becoming mindful is easier when there is less frustration, anger, or judgment involved. As stated before, these things cloud our thinking, and we lose the chance to build a connection with our kids. Every time we meet parents who complain of disobedience, we ask them how they react to situations where the child break the rules or does something that embarrassed them. Most of the parents respond with answers like giving their children cold stares, yelling, scolding, and even at times, hitting. As you may know, all these actions – the one thing we have to control, are not part of positive parenting, and they are classic indicators of frustration and anger.

We often tell parents that instead of losing their temper, they should view it as an opportunity to make things right in a calm and composed manner. That is when the kids need the acceptance of who they are from their parents. They want to be assured that, even though they messed up, their parents still love them. So grab that opportunity with both hands and make the most of it. It doesn't mean that you look over your child's mistake and misbehavior, but rather you sit them down and let them know that although they did something wrong, you aren't mad. Make it a point that the behavior they depicted is not acceptable and that you would very much appreciate it if they didn't repeat it. Tell them what your expectations are of them and ask if they would like to say something as well. The idea is to not let them feel like they are being schooled or lectured but rather being talked to with concern.

We know for a fact that almost three-fourth of parents see parenting as the biggest challenge they ever had to face, but if you do as stated above, you will soon realize that disciplining isn't as hard as it sounds. All we need is to find the right tools and use the right strategies to raise a sensible, emotionally intelligent, and well-mannered child.

If you continue to see parenting as a difficult chore, which, frankly it can be, you will keep finding it hard at every step of the way. You will feel stressed when you have to change diapers, feed your kids, and worry about what's best for them – all the while, doubting your own choices and judging your own parenting capabilities. What if we tell you that perfection is not the goal of being a better parent and that it is time we let go of the idea of "being perfect," altogether? There is no such thing as perfect parenting, as every parent faces different and unique challenges with their kids. No two kids are alike, which sadly, makes parenting a bit harder. What might have worked with your elder one might not work with your younger one.

However, what DOES work, regardless of which children it is, is mindful parenting. It all begins with accepting the things you can't control. You can't control your child's preferences and personality. Do not compare them with their siblings and peers. The fact that your child is different from their siblings and peers does not mean that you are doing something wrong. When we begin to look at mindful parenting as the ability to become fully present and pay attention to our kids with compassion, kindness, and respect, we begin to love them even more naturally because we see them for their uniqueness, for who they are and not who we wish them to be.

Practicing Mindful Parenting: A Guide for Beginners

Keep in mind that while we suggest mindful parenting, it isn't synonymous with becoming the perfect parents to your kids. There will be times when you will fail and rethink the advice you took from this book. Learning to be mindful and accepting the situation at hands is s a learning process. You can expect it to be hard, but not impossible. You are going to get the hang of it eventually and figure out the techniques that best work for you and your kid/kids.

Before we get to this insider's guide, we must tell you that, as beginners, it is going to take some patience on your part and a whole lot of practice. Some days will be good and the others not so much. You may give in to your emotions some days and some days learn to control them. But keep in mind that every step of the way, you will be left with two choices – either to react spontaneously or to pause, reflect, then respond.

Taking a moment to contemplate before responding is the essence of becoming a mindful parent. You pay attention to what's happening in the present and not get carried away by your emotions. Throughout the process of becoming mindful, you will learn to let go of any shame and guilt about the actions of your past and focus on dealing with the ones you feel presently. You simply learn to accept things as they happen rather than doing anything about it or attempting to change or ignore them. But that doesn't mean you can't or won't get angry. You will still sense the negative feelings brewing up inside you like a fresh pot of coffee; however, you will stop responding to them mindlessly.

Below are some of the basic steps you need to keep a note of when adopting mindful parenting.

Give Your Child Your Full Attention

Sometimes, all one needs is an ear to tell things to. Be that person for your child. You must be wondering, isn't that all that we do? But amidst all the things, this is the one thing we aren't doing. We may think we are, but we are prone to multitasking with an attention span of fewer than eight seconds. Even when we do sit down to hear their thoughts, imaginations, and ideas, we fail to listen to what they are truly trying to tell us.

Listening is an essential step to becoming a mindful parent. This is the first habit you need to adopt. Try to understand what they mean when they are telling things. They may not always use the best choice of words or use no words at all, but that is when we need to focus on their body language and actions to understand what they are trying to say. For example, a toddler crying in a stroller or seeming uneasy means that they may want to get out of it. Or, maybe they're hungry, or just tired. Their crying and uneasiness are what you need to interpret and act upon.

When you begin to listen and pay attention, you learn how to respond better.

Accept Who They Are (Even When They Annoy You)

Judging someone based on their actions, behavior, or mood is the easiest thing to do in the world. Sometimes, we do the same with our kids and in a rather harsh manner. Some days they will be hard to handle. Those are the days when you have to stay patient and not give in to your negative feelings. After all, ask yourself this: does punishment by scolding, for example, really work? Generally, it gets your children attention; however, long term, would scolding foster a good relationship between you and your child? If your answer is no, then we have to accept the fact that sometimes your child's behaviour will deviate from your expectation and your responsibility is to accept and find the cause of their behavior.

If they are being hard, annoying or needy, don't tell them to act older than their age and "get it together before dad comes home." Don't scare them into changing who they are. Some kids just need an extra dose of love and care. Offer them that and notice how the acting out will cease after some time. Acceptance of their feelings and letting them know that you understand what they are going through is an instant trust-builder. As a mindful parent, you need to be their rock and support them.

Feel What They Are Feeling

This means putting yourself in their shoes sometimes and viewing the world how they are viewing it. If they don't want to get into the bath and cry their eyes out, imagine how they are feeling. Ask yourself, why would they not want to take a bath? Are they scared? If they cry over not finding their favorite blanket before bedtime, imagine what they must be going through. What is your usual reaction when you can't find something important to you? You feel a mixture of anger, frustration, and tears. They are feeling the same. They just don't know how to handle it appropriately. Again, when you try to understand their point of view, your response to any given situation changes, and you become more compassionate and caring.

Dealing With Frustrations and Anger Using Mindfulness

You often find yourself in the fight or flight mode throughout the day. This can make you look at your kid as the enemy because you are too swept with anger to think things through and deal with the problem they are facing. Sometimes, the anger gets to the point that some parents consider physical punishment if the situation continues. Our stress causes our muscles to go all tense, breathing to quicken and our pulse to race. It becomes almost impossible to stay in control as the Hulk in all of us is ready to rip off its clothes and throw its wrath upon the enemy.

But, take a breath. Even though you may get angry - very angry - with your child, there's no reason to act on that anger, be it with words or with other actions that exert your power over your child.

Even when yelling at your child seems like a solution for anger relief, it really isn't. As their parent, you are foremost their guardian. Your role is to keep them safe from all the things they are scared of and not become another person or thing that your child is afraid of.

This leads to the second rule to becoming a mindful parent, and that is to not react in a state of anger. No sane decisions are made when one is angry. The only thing that follows when reacting in anger is immense regret, which is something we don't want you to go through. So instead of giving in to the urge of "teaching" your kid a lesson then and there, opt to discipline them at a later time when you are at a higher mental state. Your child isn't going anywhere. You can always sit them down whenever you want and instil some wisdom in them. You might be wondering, "easier said than done," and that's true. It will take practice. But trust us on this. To make it easier for you, we are listing some of the best mindfulness practices to adopt when you feel frustrated or angry about your child.

Address the Elephant in the Room

The first exercise involves acknowledgement. Everything has to start from you accepting the negative feelings as they come instead of running from them. Give yourself a verbal reason as to why you are feeling the way you are and what is causing it. If it is your kid that is making you angry, say this to yourself, "I am angry because he/she did [action]."

Next, analyze those emotions. Find out where they are coming from and are they truly related to the present situation or just some venting over something else? Here, you must identify if the emotions are in line with what is happening and whether this is how you should be reacting or not. This calls for an analysis of how major or minor the situation is. For instance, refusing to take a bath shouldn't get you all riled up and yell at your toddler. Why? Because this isn't the first time they are refusing to bathe, and you also know it isn't going to be the last either.

So, this is really just a minor issue and something you deal with daily. It shouldn't rile you up to the extent that results in shouting. If it does, then there is something else that is concurrently bothering you, and perhaps you bottled it up earlier. This means your anger is entirely about something else. This refusal, however, has tipped the glass over that was filled with anger to the brim. Now, unless you resolve that primary issue and acknowledge it, you aren't going to find a resolution to your emotional turmoil, and neither will your child understand why you're so upset.

Finally, we want you to think things through, which means we want you to inspect your reactions before they happen. The best way to do so is to imagine the situation as if it were reversed.

Imagine you were the one being shouted at. Were you expecting such an overwhelming response? How did it make you feel? When you know how the other person feels, and how you would have felt had you been in their position, you begin to think twice before addressing your anger.

The STOP Discipline

This is a rather interesting way to deal with frustration and anger. The STOP discipline refers to four different things, with each playing a critical role in helping you react to situations mindfully. Here's how you can use it to your benefit.

S: The S stands for "stop". The first step is to cease and take a pause. It entails coming to terms with what is happening and how it is affecting you. This is only possible when you detach yourself from the situation and begin to analyze your emotions.

T: The T stands for "taking a deep breath" and later exhaling slowly. Repeat this at least seven times. More oxygen in your system helps calm your racing heart – something you will need in order to focus better.

O: The O stands for "observing your reactions and emotions" once you begin breathing in and out. You should feel less tense and feel calmness spreading through your mind, body, and spirit.

P: Finally, the P stands for "proceed," which means you can respond, now that you are more aware of yourself and your emotions. Chances are, you will feel less frustrated and respond with logic instead of anger.

Ignite the Coal

This is another great practice for when you feel out of control and ready to unleash your wrath upon your little ones or anyone in general. The COAL technique includes:

Curiosity

Openness

Acceptance

Love

All of which are steps to help resolve any issue in a calm manner. It starts with you taking a few deep breaths and detaching yourself from the situation. You can either leave the room, request a few minutes of peace or simply sit down and bring your child in a hug.

Curiosity: Starting with the first step, you need to be curious in figuring out what is making you this mad. Is it just the kid, or are there other things bothering your peace of mind too?

Openness: Next, you need to try to strike a conversation with your kid in a way that doesn't invoke more crying or whining. Ask them what they need but tell them that for you to understand them better they need to pause their cry and talk to you about it. This works best with children who have some basic verbal skills. During this openness stage, you need to be open to your children's needs and pay attention without judgment. Once you are able to connect with your child and get their attention, notice the changes in their behavior and expressions. Do they stop crying? What is the tone of their voice?

Acceptance: Acknowledge and accept that little initiation with warmth and support to let them know that you understand what they need and why they need it. This is the part where you respond to them with empathy.

Love: Finally, let them know that they are loved irrespective of what they did wrong.

Notice the drastic change in their attitude when it dawns on them that their parents understand their concerns and pay attention to them. That is the kind of bond you need to nurture from an early stage so that the highest level of trust is established between the parent and the child. If this works, which most of the time it will, you will never have to worry about your child hiding stuff from you or going behind your back with something mischievous. They will begin to acknowledge your feelings too, as they know that you are forgiving and willing to listen. So they will begin to ask for things rather than crying for them. That should be the goal of every mindful activity.

Take a Nap

Sounds like a great plan, but this isn't the nap we are talking about here. Here, NAP refers to noticing, allowing, and passing on.

Let's break it down using an example. Picture this: your kid has the flu and is more emotionally sensitive than usual. Every little thing is upsetting him. They are crying over what they want to eat instead of what you made for them, not willing to change into new clothes and wanting to stay in their pajamas all day, even when they need to be laundered.

This has been going on for two days now, and you are on the verge of losing patience with them. You have tried everything to keep them calmed and help them feel as comfortable as possible while being sick, but they are refusing to take their meds and are crying non-stop. As much as your heart hurts looking at them, you just want to escape into another parallel universe because you can't take it anymore. They are pushing the limit of your patience, and you know it!

Notice: A mindful way of dealing with this situation starts with noticing the painful sensations your body experiences along with the kind of thoughts crossing your mind. They may not be all positive and uplifting, but noticing them is the first step to making things better.

Allow: Next, you have to allow these emotions and accept them without changing them. Then, you wait for them to pass on, which is the third step of this exercise.

Pass on: Allowing negative emotions to pass through your system is bidding them goodbye for good and releasing yourself from them. Remember nothing lasts forever, even negative emotions.

This acceptance practice prepares us to deal with negative feelings and emotions without running away from them. With practice, you will soon become a master of taking a NAP even in the most difficult situation.

Breathe in, Breathe Out

This is probably the oldest trick in the book, and often also the first one that comes to our minds when we hear the word mindfulness. But what we fail to understand is the importance it holds in our daily lives. It isn't something just useful when trying out some yoga poses. It is ideal in all those situations where we sense a loss of patience and frustration settling in. It is especially excellent when dealing with everyday tantrums; practicing mindful breathing daily and as many times as possible will facilitate us in handling stressful situations better.

We all are familiar with the basic mindful breathing. We start by closing our eyes and taking a deep breath until our stomach starts to ache a little. Then, we release and exhale out the trapped air slowly, and repeat the same until we feel calmness seeping inside us. This not only gives our organs an extra bout of air but also halts the production and release of chemicals like cortisol in the body, which triggers stress and anxiety. The more stress we feel, the less capable we are of controlling our emotions. And when we give in to negative emotions, they further promote the negativity. Think about it, when a kid receives a sound yelling or lecture, do they stop crying, or do they increase it a pitch further?

Blow Off Steam

Blowing off steam refers to diverting and channelling your anger to things or activities other than the thing or person that causes the anger. These activities could be going to the gym, a dance party, or singing at the top of your lung. Not many people support this form of releasing frustration as it doesn't solve the root of the problem; however, when it comes to parenting, especially with younger kids, who we want to see flourish with good habits and qualities, it can be a lifesaver. You begin by detaching yourself from the situation that is causing anger, and instead, turn to something else to let it all out. This technique works similarly to when your boxing trainer tells you to picture someone or something you hate and channel your energy to the punching bag. The idea is to not keep anything bottled up as it only complicates things further and relieves our systems of any negative emotions and feelings. However, blowing off steam doesn't damage some other thing or hurt someone else; it simply means looking for a healthy outlet for your anger and aggression.

Physical activity, like boxing, is a great cardiorespiratory workout and also a stress reducer. It causes the brain to release endorphins, the neurotransmitter that generates the sense of well-being, a.k.a. the feel-good chemical. Body movement during physical activities also helps to relieve muscle tension that accumulates from stress. Other suggestions for healthy ways to blow off steam are going for a run, calling a friend to vent about the situation, and journaling. As long as you're being responsible and mature about how you channel your negative emotion, activities like these can be very helpful. If your kids are old enough to understand, you can even tell them what you're doing: "I (Mommy/Daddy) am frustrated at the moment. I am boxing to blow off some steam so that I don't do or say something that might accidentally hurt other's feelings. Please give me fifteen minutes (or however long you need)."

Practice Self-Compassion

Treat yourself and your kids with compassion. Part of becoming more mindful begins with self-compassion, where you learn to let go of the mistakes you make as a parent and learn to love yourself. You have to stop comparing yourself with other parents and the methods they use. Not everything applies directly to you, so you have to stop thinking that you are a bad parent when your kids act out or misbehave. We are the first ones to criticize ourselves. We keep reminding ourselves that we aren't doing enough and that frustrations keep on building inside us until one day, we finally vent it out on either our partners or kids. Self-compassion, of course, isn't something that comes naturally for some of us who are perfectionists, but with practice, we can learn to have more compassion for ourselves. One technique is to use visualization. Imagine the traits or characteristics you would like to develop to be a better parent while accepting yourself and your kids where you currently are.

Here's how to practice it at home.

Start with finding yourself a comfortable and distraction-free space to sit in. Take a deep breath and let it out slowly. You can choose to keep your eyes open or closed, whichever way you prefer. Next, name the emotion you are feeling. Say it yourself out loud while continuing to take deep breaths and exhaling. Notice how your body reacts when you name the emotion. Does it tense up, loosen, or go into an uncomfortable stance? After that comes the acceptance part. Place both your hands on your heart and imagine you are holding it in between the palms of your hands. Gently caress it and visualize that you are filling your heart with love and kindness. For a more visual representation, view kindness as a bright light entering your heart and lighting up everything in the surroundings too. Continue taking deep breaths, and until you feel your body loosening up, continue visualizing that.

Once you are positive that the emotion you felt is now replaced with kindness in your heart, let your hands go back into their original position, stand up, and resume your normal daily activity. We recommend that you repeat this visualization every day so that you are kinder and more compassionate to yourself. Parenting is hard enough. You don't need to make it harder by being unkind to yourself.

Respond Instead of React

We briefly introduced you to the idea of this earlier because this is one of the most remarkable things you need to work upon to improve your relationship with your child and instil in them some ideal habits. This comes recommended by Job, Kabat-Zinn and Myla, co-authors of the book, Everyday Blessings, The Inner Work of Mindful Parenting. Throughout the book, the authors have distinguished between the two states of mind - reacting and responding. To a beginner, these may seem synonymous at first glance, but they are far from being equal.

Reacting is the state of being mindless. It usually refers to an immediate and rather irrational response resulting from one's emotions driven by attachments and expectations. We all set certain hopes and expectations with our kids, and when they fail to live up to them, we become angry and frustrated. Reacting without thinking seems like the right thing to do as we believe we have given them all the resources they need to act a certain way. Take, for instance, a kid who fails a class, and the father's first reaction is to punish their child by yelling and grounding the kid. Since the father thinks he had provided the kid with all the resources they needed to pass the class and still failed to live up to the set expectations, he thinks that his punishment is justified. However, let examine this for a minute. How are yelling and grounding beneficial to the child's educational development? Would it change the letter on the report card?

Responding, in comparison to reacting, is an act of mindfulness. It is where the individual thinks before reacting mindlessly or giving in to their first knee-jerk reaction. It involves scrutiny but free of judgment. You take some time before responding and think of the reasons why something happened and what calls for a suitable response. If we consider the example from above, the father, instead of yelling and grounding the child would think about what could have led the kid to fail, form an appropriate response that doesn't involve demotivation and then try to initiate a conversation once the response has been delivered empathetically and proactively. In this case, the child will be more willing to open up and talk about why they think they might have failed in the first place. It may be because the class was not a subject of the child's interest, or the child is being bullied at school. In both cases, the child will need the support of parents to figure out their passion or learn how to deal with peer conflicts.

Now that you have seen both reacting and responding in practice, which seems to be more promising? Which one do you think your child would prefer if they were in a similar situation? Which method do you think will nurture a mutually respectful relationship between you and your child?

Becoming Empathetic Towards Kids

This brings us to the importance of being empathetic towards children. We have become so used to spontaneously reacting that we have forgotten how to respond. Of all the things kids need the most, acceptance, care, and interest take the top three places on the stands. It is what they crave the most. They want to be accepted for who they are, even when they misbehave and act out of order. Especially then. It is like they are testing their parents to see if their love is conditional or not. Second, they need to know that they can come up to you with any concern and worry and they will be looked after. Think of caring as a blend of love and safety that every child wants to have. Lastly, they want to see their parents interested in and committed to them. They want to know if their parents are good listeners, show concern about their feelings, and value their opinions or not, no matter how stupid and naïve they are.

Give any child these three things, and they will turn out to be well-raised, decent, and mindful kids.

Now picture this being put into practice. Your kid has trouble getting dressed and getting down for breakfast on time. This has been happening for over a week now, and you are done shouting and yelling, "Breakfast is ready! Come down now, or you will miss your school bus." You want them to show some maturity and get ready on time for once. Every day, little by little, your frustration and anger are building g up, and today feels like the day when it will all come out if they don't "get down this minute." You tell them that if they don't come down this minute, you will confiscate all their toys as they are making you late for work too.

This is a very normal reaction, right? Many of us have been in a similar situation at some point in our lives too. But what you don't see is that reacting in such a manner is only relieving you of your frustration, but not getting their issues resolved. Your child still seems to have problems managing time, and your venting out isn't going to help. You are only releasing yourself of the negativity without taking into account what is happening with your kid. They are also struggling with something, i.e., getting ready, and would maybe prefer some help over yelling.

If, in this scenario, you choose to show empathy instead, it will change the whole dynamic of the current situation. How so? Showing empathy means you not only acknowledge your feelings but are also concerned about the feelings of your child. You take a moment to understand what your child is feeling. Instead of further causing them trouble and worry, you help take some of it off their shoulders by being kind and empathetic. Ask your children if they need help pick out their outfits and have their backpack ready before going to bed so that the morning routine will flow more timely and effectively. This careful responding helps you notice things you might have neglected had you chosen to react instead of responding mindfully.

So what is empathy if not a way of communicating and connecting better? It lets your kids know that their feelings are valued and taken into account as well, even when the parents don't understand their situation. It is having this knowledge that counts. Empathy suggests that you aren't alone in all this and that we are here for you. It also says that we care and feel for you and wish to make it better somehow.

Receiving this message is important for your kids as they need to hear this. It makes them feel less scared and more confident because they have strong backing. They are no longer reluctant to try something that scares them. They feel more confident in their capabilities, and that is what helps them form good, healthy habits.

Every child wants to know that they are supported and understood. This makes them stay committed and driven to their passions. When they feel that their parents aren't happy with their choices, and often regard them as amateur and senseless, they are soon to give up. Try repeatedly telling a child that playing the guitar won't help them with their grades, and one day, they will give it up. They will start believing what you have been telling them and give up on their dreams. This is one reason why psychologists hate the idea of limiting kids to choose their passions. They may never find out if they are good at something or not if never given a chance.

Secondly, empathy also helps kids become self-aware and speak up for themselves and others. When they see that their parents care and show interest, they are going to act similarly toward others. Empathy is a great quality to nurture from an early age to help children develop into emotionally-intelligent adults.

Empathy also helps one understand the cause of certain behavior. It allows the parent and the child to work as a team to resolve any obstacles together. Not to mention, when your family work as a team, it strengthens your bond and helps you two connect on a deeper level.

Although we shall discuss empathy in great depth in chapter 3, we would like to end this chapter by leaving you with the four important elements of it.

1. *See Things from Someone Else's Perspective:* The first thing empathy entails is putting your feelings and emotions aside and looking at things from someone else's perspective without judgment. Know that no one likes to act out or misbehave on purpose. Even when a child misbehaves out of the ordinary, they are trying to seek attention. This is a call for love. If they are failing at something repeatedly, they aren't deliberately trying to test your patience. They are trying their best but facing some difficulty reaching the result. Empathy is simply knowing that your child is trying their best.

2. *Stop Judging:* Similar to point #1, empathy calls for acceptance without judgment. It stops one from jumping to conclusions right away and understand what is happening. Most of

the time, we lack complete information about something or neglect the signs of distress when we see them. We don't have the time to deal with them, and hence, let things be as they are. Therefore, the second most important thing is to know what more you need to know before giving them a sentence and taking out your frustration on your children.

3. *Understand the Feelings of Others:* In this case, the feelings of your child. You have to tap deep within yourself to understand where your child is coming from. What would you have done had you been in a similar state at a similar age? Your kids, no matter small or big they are, lack the wisdom you have. They may not have everything figured out as you do, and that messes with their brain. As a result, they act out, disobey commands, and misbehave. So if there is a certain way that they are reacting, try to make sense of what they are going through and how they are processing the overwhelming feelings. This also applies to when they are overly excited about something and stop listening to you, perhaps like running in a crowded amusement park when you tell them not to. But chances are, you would have done the same at that age, so what they are feeling is quite normal. It's you who sees it as misbehavior. Maybe they are just being kids.

4. *Communicate Better:* Your goal as an empathetic listener shouldn't be to try and fix the problems your kid faces. Maybe all they need is an ear to voice out their fears and not an actual solution. Therefore, avoid trying to take the controls from them

and fix things on your own. Let them come to one themselves. All you should offer is some direction. You should just help them express themselves better and encourage them to push through it with supportive words. Use reflective phrases more where you ask them what they think would be the best thing to do in the current situation. Use comforting gestures like hugs, a pat on the back, kisses on the cheeks, and an arm around their shoulder to let them know you care, understand, and worry for them.

Chapter 3: They're Just Little People

Have you ever wondered when we stopped being kids? Did we just wake up feeling different one day? Or, did our "adult" wisdom come to us in a dream? When did so many of us stop being in awe of life and end up with a mundane 9 to 5 to make a living?

If given the opportunity, how many of us would like to go back in time like a glitch in the Matrix and be our younger selves again? Maybe not all of us want to go back to our younger selves, but many of us would agree that we want to live a carefree life. Well, sadly, Rowan and I don't hold any secret codes to a time machine, we are simply curious when do we stop being kids and become adults. When and how did we get over with all the playing and get serious about responsibilities and chores that need to be done?

Not long ago, many scholars believed that kids were nothing but miniature versions of adults. They were regarded to have the same thinking and analytical ability as a fully-grown adult. However, this wasn't true. What was true, though, was that kids were mindful. Their ability to laugh at any situation, be truly indulged in the present, and being honest were all traits that many adults aspire to possess today. Similar to laughter, mindfulness is contagious. We forget all our worries too and enjoy the present moment when surrounded by young children.

So, if the ability to be mindful is something we all had as children, then why can't we be mindful all the time? Why are we stressed 90% of the time about the things that either happened in the past or are too far along in the future? Why can't we just focus on the present and live life to the fullest? It's paradoxical that as we grow "older and wiser", many of us become more disconnected with things and the people around us and become more consumed with constant worries and problems. The life of a parent is not much different either. We are always worrying, planning, running here and there, and focusing on anything but the present. We rarely feel that we are capable of controlling our emotions and prefer to keep them suppressed. As a result, it affects all the relationships we build, even the ones with our kids.

How Are Kids Different From Us?

When we want to learn about the differences between our kids and us, we have to take into account cognitive milestones as they represent the development of a child accurately. As stated before, for many centuries, researchers believed that kids were small adults. It was in the late 20th century that scientists, via several cognitive experiments, figured that there was nothing true about that. The minds of both kids and adults functioned differently. Several attributes differ between kids and adults.

Jean Piaget's contribution to determining the different cognitive developments in kids holds valuable significance. According to Piaget, many life-long habits are learned by kids during their infancy and adolescence stages. Children are born with great thinking and exploring capabilities, which enables them to become curious and discover things on their own. From the minute they are born, they are grasping new concepts, trying to imitate behaviors and actions, and learning from their surroundings. To simplify things, he categorized the cognitive development into four distinct stages which include the Sensorimotor stage (birth to two years), Preoperational stage (from two years to seven years), Concrete stage (from seven years to eleven years), and the Formal Operational stage (from twelve years and beyond).

Mr. Piaget regarded kids as little scientists, always eager to explore the endless possibilities of ideas. Their curiosity and fascination for everyday things and how they functioned was something that held great interest to him, which is why he was such a keen observer of the development of their minds and learned how they used their brains to explore and experience things. He discovered that the more intrigued a child was about something, the bigger their knowledge span was.

In the early stages of cognitive development, all kids portray various personalities because they are used to applying all of their sensory experiences. Their ability to be mindful allows them to engage with world through different modalities fully. When a child reaches the stage of adolescence, they begin to experience many physical and mental changes. Environment and life experiences shape the type of personality the child possesses, which leads us to the Myers-Briggs personality profile—a well-known way of identifying what category of personality type each of us falls under. Let's take a look and learn what your little one's personality is like and see a rough but predictable draft of how they are going to grow up.

Children and Their Distinct Personalities

Many of us believe that babies are born with a clean slate. We feel that whatever we write on that board will be the traits they pick up. All this goes well until the next one arrives, and we feel confused as to why our parenting methods no longer apply to them in the same way they did to the first child. It feels like they have a mind of their own, and nothing we say or do gets imprinted on them. This is when it dawns on us that not every child is the same, and every child has a distinct personality they bring within themselves. We have all labelled our kids resembling someone from the paternal or maternal side in terms of habit with things like, "You are just like your Aunt Judy. She loved to play tennis when she was young", or "You are growing up to be just like your grandfather. He used to nibble on his food the same way you do."

Therefore, with each child bringing a set of completely different personalities to the table, our parenting games need to be purposeful and strategic. We need to incorporate distinct methods that not only work for both children but also tailor to their unique needs and interests. So, keep this in mind, it is time we assess all the various personality types, so we can better understand our kids.

The Myers-Briggs assessment is divided into eight categories, which further subdivide into sixteen personality types revealing your child's innate profile. It is designed for people of all ages, including adults. Employers sometimes use this assessment for hiring or for placing employees with teams that most suitable for them. Each personality type is represented by four letters paired together, and each letter is a unique characteristic in itself. The following are the eight basic personality types (paired) we shall discuss in greater detail below.

1. Extravert and Introvert
2. Sensing and Intuition
3. Thinking and Feeling
4. Judging and Perceiving

Extrovert and Introvert

To determine where a child's core energy comes from, we look at two variables – external and internal. Are they the ones to come out of their classrooms last, or are they the first ones to burst through the doors, pumped up with energy, and ready to tell you everything that happened that day? Does the thought of going to a cousin's house excite them, or do they prefer to stay back at home? An extroverted child seems always to be on fire and fueled by adrenaline. An introverted kid, on the other hand, will be reluctant to open up or be social. Extroverts are party animals and enjoy the company of others, whereas introverts are less excited about meeting people and often throw tantrums to prevent them from going altogether. Introverts like their own space and frequent changes tend to upset them.

Extrovert

Social interactions energize extroverts. Extroverts are often the kids that get along with everyone they meet for the first time. They are not hesitant to engage in a social setting, and their curiosity to know everything about all subject matter is what makes them such active and action-packed individuals. They strive for chaos and are not ones to be made to sit in a corner and observe others. They want to be included. Their lack of calmness sometimes affects their ability to concentrate, as they are easily distracted. Due to their tendency to get sidetracked, they don't often make for the brightest of students in the traditional academic setting; however, they can achieve greatness if taught things creatively. They enjoy learning that is hands-on and comes with physical engagement. They are more likely to learn in classrooms with fewer students, as it allows them to engage in conversations actively.

Introvert

Introverts are the opposite of extroverts. They are energized by their inner world of thoughts, reflection, and contemplation. They are often average learners and require time and space to do things their way. Many of them love reading and writing, which makes them great students when they are interested in the subject. Their learning style is often suited for traditional classrooms where peers and teachers present them with long lectures. They want to work in a corner and be left by themselves to work on their task. They are rarely open and expressive, but when they are, they prefer it happening one-on-one or a small group. As kids, they prefer discipline and routines, as they find comfort in predictability and consistency. Compared to extroverts, they tend to be more mindful, as they take their sweet time in cultivating responses rather than speaking their mind without thinking.

Sensing or Intuition

An ideal way to determine which personality type your child possesses is to ask them to remember an event or place they recently visited. Notice what they remember about it the most. Is it the ambiance and the mood or the smell, sounds, or colors? See what words they use to describe the event too. Sensing descriptors are more concerned about how the event was carried, and the intuitive descriptors are more concerned about the various elements such as the table decorations, layout, and theme of the place.

Sensing

To be clearer, kids with a sensing personality use all their senses to gather information. They are more receptive and keen observers. They are inspired by visually appealing details and generally are good listeners. They have a good memory and recall things faster. They also like to abide by the rules and play safe. Having a kid with a personality type in this category means you have someone who wishes to adhere to the set rules and regulations and rarely has the urge to challenge them. They also like to have things planned for the whole day, such as knowing the time for a bath, the time to play or nap. They crave structure, concrete facts, and organization in all things.

Intuition

These people use their intuition to guide them through things. They are curious beings and creative. They are, at times, quite hasty as they tend to miss important facts and thus aren't the type to be caged in with rules. Their curiosity keeps them on their toes all day, and they are the ones exploring things and asking questions. They are little innovators and don't always run to their parents or siblings for guidance. They prefer dealing with things on their own and thus will keep on attempting at one thing for hours until they get it right. They are also energetic and more active.

Thinking or Feeling

Does your kid seem to be motivated by facts or emotions? Thinkers are objective. They are ruled by their head instead of their heart and value truth over tact. They think through things logically and reach sane and rational decisions. Feelers, on the other hand, are subjective. They think from the heart and are more empathetic toward others feelings. Feeling people judge situations and others based on feelings and extenuating circumstances. They make decisions based on principles and values.

Thinking

These kids prefer deciding things based on logic. If it is their turn to enjoy the toy, they will snatch it from their friends rather than paying any heed to the feelings of their friend. They need logic and reasoning for everything that a parent says and won't comply with something without one. Although they are great at dealing with problems on their own and finding ways to resolve issues, their impersonal character and lack of empathy and compassion can, at times, come out too firm on people. In school, they are often the ones with strong opinions and need solid reasoning to change their mind. They don't understand the concept of favoritism and aspire to be treated equally. Therefore, even if you tell them that their little sibling needs more attention because they are sick, they are going to try and challenge you at it.

Feeling

As suggested earlier, feelers are gentle and compassionate. They take into account the feelings of others and their own. They make decisions based on how they feel about the circumstances rather than what they think about it. Due to their receptive nature, they are easily hurt by others; however, this doesn't always mean that they set themselves up for failure. Feeling people are great supporter, mentor, and advocate. They are mostly the ones liked by the majority of other people. They get distressed when they sense interpersonal friction and favor harmony.

Judging or Perceiving

Is your child someone who likes structure and order in everything, or is he/she an individual that prefers to go with the flow of things? Kids who fall in the judging category like to plan things out beforehand whereas kids in the perceiving category like to let things go with the flow and are more flexible with unexpected changes. Judging personality in this instance doesn't mean that your child is judgmental. It refers to how your child prefers to deal with day-to-day activity.

Judging

Kids with this personality type prefer to exercise control over everything in their lives. They are less open-minded to change, decisive and well-organized in general. They grow up to become highly responsible adults as they are all about meeting deadlines and having daily action plans. They crave structure in their lives and prefer single-tasking. You have a kid with the judging trait if they watch TV first and later eat dinner because they seek closure and enjoy completing tasks.

Perceiving

Kids who fall under perceiving category are rather spontaneous and prefer not being caged in with any set plans and deadlines. They aren't a big fan of schedules and routines either as they like adventure and spontaneity in life. They like to have all the resources and information they need to make decisions. They grow up to be great at multitasking. Their spontaneity in life makes them good at reacting better in emergencies when things don't go according to the plan. However, the only drawback of their personality is that they are better at starting things but not so much at completing them. They tend to view deadlines as mere suggestions and they like to keep their option opens.

Importance of Personality Analysis

The reason we have provided you with these insights about each personality type is so that you can understand where your children are coming from when they are behaving in a certain way. Although a child's personality should never be the reason for behaving inappropriately, it can be beneficial for parents to understand their nature, so they have a better chance of dealing with them in a much more tactical and calm way. Every child is different, so it can be quite overwhelming for one parent to deal with multiple kids of different ages and different personalities.

For example, a child with an introverted personality may resist going to crowded spaces because they find it hard to mingle like other kids and, instead, opt for a quiet spot in the corner. However, when parents force that child to mingle and get comfortable with other kids, that is where the problem arises. This occurs when the parent isn't concerned about the personality of the child or isn't much aware. However, a conscious parent will be better able to understand the feelings of their child and will avoid forcing them to engage in activities that might deem conflicting the nature of the particular children and instead foster them to grow and develop skills that align with their personality types.

Similarly, if a parent knows that their child is someone who prefers sticking to strict routines, they might not try to upset the children's routines by making swift changes. Instead, they might try to make those changes as subtle as possible so that it doesn't bother their kid or hurt their feelings. We can go on with many more examples, but hopefully, you have understood the memo and see why paying attention to their personality and trying to parent them accordingly can be a tool for better parenting. When the child doesn't feel threatened, pushed or forced into doing something that isn't them, a stronger and healthier relationship can be built.

Enter Mindful Listening

One of the most effective ways to handle tantrums and outrages from kids, without losing your own sense of calm, is to listen to them mindfully so that you don't miss out on the early signs of distress and discomfort. It is always best to run ideas and plans with kids before you try something to implement something novel. For instance, if you want them to clean their room after they are done playing, it is best to address your concern prior. Chances are when kids know what is expected of them; they behave better. We used the same tactic on all of our kids, and trust us, they made less mess knowing they will have to clean up afterwards - before dinner time! If they listen to you and you listen to them, things will run much more smoothly - most of the time.

The art of listening is an underrated one, especially in parenting. However, those who have had more than one child will know what we are talking about. Kids have a mind of their own and, often, many things they say or do don't make much sense. However, when matters are communicated efficiently, and both the involved parties know what the other expected of them, there is less chance of conflict and thus, an even lesser chance of losing your temper.

Listening allows you to give your child your uninterrupted attention when they are telling you things and showing them that you care. It involves using all of your senses to let them know that you are present and you understand them. Your verbal response should align with your body language and the actions you take. Sometimes, it isn't hard for a kid to know that they are being bribed into something and that the parent isn't sincere. False hopes and fake promises are the biggest blunders parents make. Therefore, your actions should also be in line with your words, to show sincerity.

When listening mindfully, you must ensure that you are listening without judgment and with patience. You must also show the utmost interest in the conversation, no matter how senseless it seems. If you aren't mindful, it will be very easy for you to lose focus and become distracted. Half listening to your kid will tell your child that you aren't fully engaged or that their issue does not matter. Not to mention, you might miss out on some important detail that was the essence of the whole conversation. Failing to listen to that means you won't be able to respond empathetically and provide a practical solution for their problem or inquiry.

Did you know that an average person remembers only 25% of what they just heard someone say a few minutes ago (Nichols & Stevens, 1957)? This means that our mind has a tendency to be distracted. If we are not paying attention, important pieces of information might get jumbled up. Now imagine being a parent and being the sole provider, guide, mentor, maid, nutritionist, guard, and companion of someone. Imagine the number of conversations going on in the house and at the office during work. It seems impossible to be handled them all with the same level of attentiveness, right?

We all have limited time and energy in a day. Hence, we must prioritize what is important. We, as parents, should invest time and energy at home as much as we do at work. One reason why kids these days feel less supported is that they think their parents aren't giving them the attention and time they deserve. So often we hear children mention about their parents bringing work home or they are checking work email or picking up work phone even on vacation. Therefore, to avoid your children perceiving you as disinterested in their matters and making your children feel like a second priority to your work, learn to become a mindful listener. Be present in front of your children. Look into their eyes when you communicate with them. When you are present, you can address your children's concerns before they become issues big enough to throw you off your parenting game.

Why do you need to become a mindful listener? Well, the perks are quite convincing. For starters, when you listen to your child mindfully, you allow yourself to be fully in the moment, all ears, which means you can hear the message being delivered to you. You can put a stop to all those wandering thoughts that rush through your mind, giving you a moment of complete solitude. This makes the speaker feel valued, heard, and most importantly, cared for. Mindful listening also allows you to grasp what has been told before passing any judgments. This way you have more time to absorb it all in first and then form a response.

This encompasses more than just hearing something but rather, understanding it. When you listen mindfully, you don't only listen to what has been shared with you but also make sense of the facial expressions, tone, and body language. This can further facilitate a parent to interpret what is being told and then form better and encouraging responses. Finally, mindful listening doesn't involve interruptions in between; the listener is supposed to listen without interrupting the speaker so that the speaker's train of thought isn't broken. Interruptions may cause your children to hesitate and sensor themselves. Thus, they were not able to fully express their conflicting emotions, leading to an emotional build-up that later can be detrimental to their mental and emotional state.

According to Dr. Larissa G. Duncan, an associate professor of Human Development and Family Studies at the University of Wisconsin-Madison, parents who are accepting and aware of their child's needs and wants are far more satisfied with the kind of relationship they have with their child and also tend to avoid cycles of dysfunctional parenting behavior.

Other studies also reveal that mindful listening helps kids handle challenges more effectively and be more compassionate when responding to others (Hanceroglu, 2017). This is something you can and should teach your children from an early age by setting a good example for them. Take a look at what mindfulness looks like when put into practice below.

What Mindful Listening Looks Like

When initiating a conversation, be present physically and mentally. You don't want to make your child think that you are distracted, in a rush, or uninterested. If they sense this, they will stop coming to you with their problems and choose to stay quiet. This will impact the way they communicate with others too. Therefore, remind yourself that once you have committed to hearing them out, they become your #1 priority. Don't let them think otherwise.

Secondly, if you are busy or think that you are too distracted or out of control to have a decent conversation, maybe choose a later time to have it. Again, the idea is to lend them not just an ear but your heart and mind too. Therefore, if you think that this important conversation can take place at some other time or place that is more appropriate, let them know that. However, make it a point to ensure that they know you aren't just shushing them off but rather want to give them your undivided attention.

If you had been distracted or engaged in some other activity like watching TV or looking at your phone, switch it off or set it aside. Nothing will hurt the speaker more when they feel that the listener is not interested in what they are trying to say, and instead distracted by electronic devices. In this case, if your child thinks that you are more interested in your social media updates than you are in them, then they will feel disrespected. It gives them the impression that what they have to say holds little value in the eyes of their parents, and therefore, there is no point in sharing it.

Repeat things but rephrase when needed. In other words, take what your child has said to you, and put them into your own words. When done mindfully, both the speaker and listener feel like they are on the same page. This also helps the speaker know that they have been listened to carefully and that you care about what they've said.

Using your own words to repeat back what has been said also builds understanding between both parties and tells the speaker that they can move on with the rest of their conversation. In simpler terms, it shows the speaker that the message has been received.

Encourage the child to be more open and comprehensive. The more information you have, the more equipped you will be at assessing their condition and coming up with a solution. To encourage them, you don't necessarily have to use words. You can simply smile and nod. You can ask for more information if they seem to be emotionally open to let you in on more (in case they aren't crying). This shows that you are genuinely interested and seeking more information so that you can help them better. It also tells them that their words and concerns hold value, which makes them feel confident and more willing to share.

You two should be on the same physical level. This means if they are standing, you should be too. If they are on the ground, that's where you need to be as well. Don't talk down to them as it could come off as if you are looking down on them. It may also suggest an authoritarian pose, and that is the last thing your kid needs. They are coming to you as a friend, and that is what they should feel like. Aim to maintain steady eye contact with them too. When you two are on the same level, it increases their level of comfort too.

Don't interrupt, but if you do, apologize immediately. Cutting your children off in the middle of a statement by correcting them or offering them advice without hearing them out completely is, again, disrespectful. Allow your children to finish their statement before contributing to the dialogue. Trying not to interrupt your children can be hard when what they are saying does not seem rational to you. However, if you catch yourself interrupting your child, as stated before, apologize quickly and ask them to continue.

Sometimes, we know where the conversation is going. We start to think about possible conclusions. When we have a few ideas in mind, it is very easy to blurt them out without letting the other person finish their thought. This is against the rules of mindful listening. You must, at all times, be patient and let your child say what they are saying even if you have already heard about their dilemmas a thousand times before today. The idea is to encourage them to speak their mind and not act like a know-it-all. Try to stay open-minded and let the tiny speaker finish before suggesting things. Once they are done, take some time to process things and formulate a response accordingly. Even if you have the solution figured out the minute they start the conversation, simply pause before you respond, and take the time to show them that you are genuinely listening and want to help.

Before forming a final response, during that brief pause, repeat all that had been told to you in an inquisitive tone. Keep asking them if you have heard them correctly so that you avoid any misunderstandings. Keep most of your questions open-ended. Asking for more clarity and information by asking open-ended questions is another great way to listen mindfully as it encourages the speaker to go into the depth of things rather than leaving you with surface-level information to form a response. Furthermore, keeping your questions open-ended also means there is room for more dialogue to occur in the future.

Avoid finishing the sentences of the speaker. You want to hear the whole story before contributing your input. You want them to express their concerns without being cut-off in the middle. Completing the sentences of the speaker for them can change the direction of the conversation, and the speaker may feel little control over it. This is both discouraging and degrading.

Stay mindful of your expressions, sensations, and body language. If the conversation is making you feel uncomfortable, it is best not to let your body language deter your children from going into further details. If the conversation is uncomfortable to you, it surely is significantly more difficult for your children to share. The fact that your child musters up the courage to share it to you, the least you could do is to listen and support them. You should stay calm throughout the conversation and think with an open mind, even when you don't agree with half of the things being told to you.

Mindful Listening Techniques for Stressed Parents

Sometimes, the very act of listening is stressful. It involves engagement and concentration and, really, who has the time for it when our schedules are running jam-packed? But it isn't always a lack of time; sometimes we just don't know how to do it. We have an idea of how to listen and what mindful dialogue is; however, to really execute it can be a different story. The initiation and setting for the conversation have to be right so that it doesn't feel staged or forced. It has to happen naturally where the speaker feels welcomed to talk and contribute. Below are three different ways to get the communication going while making it seem natural.

You Go Next…

In this mindful listening exercise, the speaker and the listener set a time of the day to sit down and talk about something. The best time for communication is when both participants feel awake and fresh, calm and attentive. To begin, start by discussing maybe how stressful things have been for you lately, and how tough the work was at the office. The idea is to get them interested first in your own story and then share some of their concerns, too. See if they are willing to contribute and open up with you. If not, ask them if their school is as hectic also. Later, probe further by asking things like if they have to deal with bullying schoolmates or irksome friends similar to your coworker at the office, etc. You get the point.

Make this one-on-one session a routine. Set a few rules, such as one partner gets to say their share uninterrupted for three minutes. Only then can the next partner can share their thoughts and troubles. You can also discuss your relationship, such as what things your child does that bothers or hurts you, and they can tell you what bothers them about you vice versa. This way, you will notice a significant change in their attitude towards you and you both will find yourself with less conflicting opinions than before.

Since all kids want to impress and please, they will also avoid deliberately pushing your buttons in an attempt to frustrate you.

Bottle Up…

This exercise involves some craftwork on your part, but hey, you can always have your kid/kids join in and help. This idea comes from the Pixar movie, *Inside Out*, with emotion bottles, each labelled for a different emotion (Marschel, 2019). Since kids aren't always verbal when they are mad and prefer to stay silent, how can you get them talking and listen mindfully to their concerns? Introduce emotion bottles. Make use of empty or old plastic bottles and label each one with an emotion. For "angry," you can add a red solution to the bottle as red usually depicts anger. You can also print out a mad expression or emoji to stick to it. You can have more bottles for "sad," "happy," "excited" or "afraid," etc.

Whenever the child feels an overwhelming emotion but doesn't want to talk about it openly, ask them to pick up an emotion bottle that they can currently relate to. Whichever container they choose will give you various ideas to deal with that emotion. For example, if they select the red bottle, it means that they are angry. Once you know, you have multiple choices. You can either let them have some personal space or try to start a conversation.

You see, this is also a form of mindful listening. It may not involve verbal expression or sharing of issues. It still gives you an overall idea of how to deal with it. You accept their emotions and don't judge them.

Validate Me, Please…

This is more of a tip than an actual exercise and involves the sharing of opinions, without being judged. Validation from parents builds confidence in kids, and they become better at pursuing new things. Validation from kids helps parents know that they are doing their best and raising good kids. So, in a way, it works both ways and benefits everyone in the end.

Again, make it a habit to discuss rather than fight about anything and everything. As a parent, you should aim to get things cleared out verbally in a calm and composed manner to prevent any major dramas and nagging. Let your kids know that you are always there to listen to whatever bothers them. Let them know that they can always come to you with their problems and that you will be all ears without judging their choices.

Promise them that whatever you will offer as a response will be a mere suggestion to improve on the existing idea of something, and not judgment. When you give them advice, be prepared that sometimes your children may not take your suggestions and decide to do their own thing. It can be hard for you as a parent when you know that their ideas and solutions can hurt them, or cause pain, but think of it as a process of trial and error. If it's a minor decision that does not have a long effect or put them in danger and that the lesson from the mistake can be an essential part of your child's development, let your children make that mistake. Even when they do get hurt after doing what they wanted to do, they will still know that you tried to help them earlier and thus would think of turning to you for future advice. That is how you cultivate trust.

Chapter 4: Parents are People Too

Since it all starts with who you are as a parent and what values you want your kid to grow up with, one of the most important aspects of parenting is self-care. Self-care involves taking ownership of your mental, emotional, and physical wellbeing. It is about putting yourself first and giving your body and mind the nourishment it needs. People often are willing to do more for people they care about than they would have done for themselves, and that's a bad mindset to have. Yes, your children are your priority, but you are your children's foundation. If you have a poor self-care habit and you are not able to be your best self, then you are setting a similar example for your children. If you are aware of the negative impact poor self-care can have on you, you will never want your kids to learn bad self-care habits from you. But before we get to that, below is a bit of a pep talk to convince you to give self-care a try.

You Are a Person First

What if we told you that you don't always have to be a parent? What if we told you that you are a person first and then a parent? Parenthood sometimes muddles the difference between the two, and we see both identities as one. But they aren't one. You have to invest in your personal growth, too. Sure, your kid's life seems the most important thing right now, but trust us, they will figure out most of it on their own. They might seek suggestions, but they will be doing most of the work themselves. A lot of parents get so invested in the lives of their kids that they forget to be their own person as well. We all have some physical, emotional, and social needs. Having any of these needs unmet stresses us out. How often has it happened that you just want to leave everything behind and be somewhere new? Of course, your conscience won't allow you to drop everything, but if you are feeling this, it is a sign that you have been neglecting your personal needs for a long time.

Don't get us wrong, there are many perks of becoming a parent, but you have to take care of yourself first. How can you expect to take care of your children and your family if you don't care about yourself? Just an idea to think about for now. The only enemy here is the society which expects us to believe that our life should revolve around our kids only. We fear that we would be perceived as selfish or as "bad parents" if we do something for our own pleasure. Some of us even feel ashamed about wanting to do things for ourselves.

Other parents find it surprising that we even thought about such a thing, but trust us, you don't have to listen to what anyone else thinks. Your health should always be your primary concern. Other people aren't the ones helping you with the kids. They aren't the ones fulfilling family demands. They aren't the ones taking your children to parks when you don't have an ounce of energy left in you. They aren't the ones tending to your kid's needs when they are sick and cry all night. They aren't the ones waking up in the middle of the night, changing diapers, and feeding the infant. YOU ARE! So don't let them bully you into thinking that wanting something for yourself every once in a while is selfish.

You are not committing a sin, if, at times, you feel like fulfilling your needs first and then your kids. You shouldn't be ashamed or feel guilty about asking for some "me" time. It is your right by all means, and everyone around you should respect that.

Self-Care and Its Role in Parenting

Self-care is any activity that results in making us feel whole and improve our well-being, whether it's our mental, physical, and emotional state. It is a way to deal with the exhaustion that comes with everyday work. Since we view parenting as a full-time job, with no sick days, it can become quite monotonous and draining.

This is why you must always find the time to invest in yourself and deal with the challenges that come with being a parent. Self-care practices have been associated with reducing stress and alleviating symptoms of anxiety and depression. When we nourish our bodies with the right nutrients, it performs better too.

There are some misconceptions regarding what self-care is and isn't. Before we move onto the practices to self-care, let's have a look at what self-care isn't so that you don't mistake it for something other than looking after one's self.

Self-care isn't forced - but, it is something that we have to be deliberate about in order for it to happen. It's another part of mindfulness. We have to be mindful of how we're feeling and what we need to do to take care of ourselves. It could be as simple as taking a quiet bubble bath, going to the spa, having coffee with friends, and getting out of the house for just a bit. At its core, self-care involves spending your time doing things that make you happy. In the wise words of Agnes Wainman, it shouldn't be something that drains your spirits or energy but rather refuels it.

Secondly, self-care isn't a selfish act. It doesn't mean attending to one's needs without any consideration about anyone else. But, it is about knowing what choices you need to make to take care of yourself so that you can take care of others. If you're exhausted, frustrated, and tired, you can't really be there for other people. As stated before, self-care is nourishment for your body and soul. It stems from the idea that if one doesn't feel cared for, they are less likely in a position to help others. Therefore, you have to fill your own cup first, because you can start filling other people's cup.

Five Areas of Self-Care

One of the most common reasons parents come up with when we suggest self-care practices for reducing frustrations and controlling anger is that they don't have the time for it. Then we bring out the big guns and tell them that they don't need to plan extensively for it, as we aren't suggesting packing your bags and going on a solo journey (although we could). It usually means making the most of the available time you have on your hands when your kids are either asleep or not around. It simply requires some time management skills on your part, and it is completely up to you to decide how much time you are willing to allot for yourself and when.

You start by finding something that truly lightens up your day. It can be an activity or hobby you used to love a while ago or something that adds value to your life, like learning a new skill or doing volunteer work. You might feel like this is not achievable; however, you just have to take a leap of faith and give it a try. You will be astonished by how carving out a little time for yourself daily makes a difference in your day.

There are five different levels or categories of self-care. Each demonstrates a distinct need, and ideally, meeting all these needs should be a priority in your life. The reason we are discussing this in such great depth is that we want you to use these five categories to create a to-do list of activities that fall under each category and start making time for them.

Sensory

Sensory care, as the name suggests, refers to taking care of your sense. Sensory care is the activation of one or more of the senses, including taste, smell, vision, hearing, and touch. It can range from something as simple as a hand massage with scented lotion or listening to a playlist of favorite music to more complicated activities designed to provide a sensory experience. Whatever you do, be present and ensure that you are in a calm and stress-free environment. Practicing mindful sensory care will allow you to focus on the present moment and let go of any limiting or negative thoughts about your past or future.

You should aim to pick activities or interests that involve all of your senses and notice which ones you are most responsive too.

Emotional

Emotional self-care refers to the attainment of stable emotional health. This entails the management of your emotions and how you control them. Again, managing your negative emotions can alleviate stress and symptoms associated with anxiety and depression. Aim for activities that arouse certain emotions and see how you react to them. You can engage in activities that enhance your mood, or you can even attempt things that make you angry, sad, or guilty. Intentionally provoking negative feelings will help you recognize your physiological response to these emotions, subsequently helping you to learn to manage them better over time and not become overwhelmed by them. As a parent whose goal is to avoid unleashing anger and frustration on our child, emotional self-care can be a great way to achieve this.

While trying out the activities that you are unhappy or angry, know that they aren't always bad. Had you never experienced those emotions first-hand, you would have never noticed what pure joy or happiness felt like. Therefore, stop looking at negative emotions as something bad or unwanted and embrace and accept them as they come.

Social

Social self-care involves a connection with others to share your happiness, concerns, and grief with. We tell our clients to view it as something of equal importance as our physical needs because social support is crucial to our well-being. It doesn't matter if you are an introvert or extrovert; we all have a few close friends or partners we are comfortable opening up to. The goal should be spending quality time with them and talking about things that affect you – both positively and negatively. Additionally, it takes off some of the pressure that comes with parenting, and you see that you aren't the only one facing challenges. Sharing your experiences with other parents may help you realize that you are not the only person experiencing the issues you are facing with your children. Maybe other parents may have an effective solution or helpful advice for your problems.

Spiritual

Know that spirituality doesn't only have to do with believing in a deity, nor is it necessarily tied to religious practice. Paying attention to our spiritual health involves getting in touch with our core values, cultures, and traditions as well. It is about doing things that are fulfilling and help us see ourselves as part of humanity. It is about feeding your soul, rather than just your mind or body, with what matters to you the most. Some people prefer practicing spirituality through meditation, chanting, journaling, etc. Others may prefer something more socially interactive, like doing yoga, joining local hiking group and spending time in nature, volunteering in the community etc. If you care about elderly people, you may choose to volunteer at a nursing home. Spiritual practices do not need to be related to any religious tradition. You are simply doing good for the sake of good. There is no hidden agenda, and you aren't pretending to do something you are not interested in. So in a way, it is more about finding a purpose in your life that makes your life meaningful and connected to humanity.

Physical

Finally, we have physical self-care, which refers to taking care of your body through adequate sleep, healthy and nutritious food (for you and your family), exercising, and staying fit. You'll find that when you take care of your body, your body takes care of you. When you eat in an overall healthy way, you have much more energy to spend quality time with your family and with yourself. You will also be modelling healthy habits and healthy relationships with food by keeping things in moderation and sticking with a generally healthy lifestyle.

Best Self-Care Strategies for Busy Parents

The second you become a parent, your whole life seem to revolve around looking after your little bundle of joy. It is very natural to lose sight of your own needs and put theirs first. But as stated before, you can't keep suppressing your needs for a long time as this can only result in more frustration and exhaustion on your part. Therefore, here are some great self-help strategies ideal for parents to ensure they don't neglect their personal needs. Because at the end of the day, you have to take care of yourself so that you can be a better parent for your little human.

Meditate

Meditation, even if it is for a few minutes every day, can allow you to stay rejuvenated. With so many guided meditation apps and online videos, you no longer have to learn how to do it but simply follow the advice. Even five minutes of daily meditation can help clear your mind and relieve your body of any worries and problematic thoughts. It can serve to be the perfect start to your day and keep you calm and your mind less cluttered.

Take a Digital Detox

We are so used to picking up our phones every few minutes, browsing social media apps so mindlessly, and spending way too much time surfing through the many channels on our TV or laptop that we don't even realize how self-harming that is. Addiction to phones is a real thing, and we have little idea of how drastically it is affecting our health and immune systems. Think about it, when was the last time you put your phone down and left it there for hours at a time? Even in the middle of the night, if we wake up to tend to our kids, we also pick up our phones to check for any new notifications on it.

What also tends to happen is that we expose ourselves to a lot of negativity when we're online, either via our phone or computers. We often see headlines filled with negative news that show society at its worst. Subconsciously, this can stress ourselves out. Rowan and I have a mutual friend who spends most of their day watching and reading political news. And guess what? He's almost always angry and upset. He talks about politics all the time, and how this congressperson does this and that party does that. Over time, this not only affects his daily mental state but his social interactions with others. It changes his interactions with his wife and his children. His family feels that his political anger and frustration was unintentionally misdirected towards them on multiple occasions.

What we suggest is a detox or cleanse. Start with limiting the amount of time spent on your phones and computers. Whenever you're tempted to take a sneak peek, engage yourself elsewhere. You don't have to reply to every message right away or reply to work emails outside of office hours. Keep in mind, also, that the blue light of your cell phone can disrupt your normal sleep cycle—the light halts the production of melatonin, which is the chemical that induces sleep.

Practice Mindfulness

This has been emphasized enough already. We feel like if we talk about it any further, you will close the book and review it as repetitive. However, we just want to let you know that the reason we keep reminding you about mindfulness is that it has been a game-changer, at least in the lives of many people who have come to us seeking parenting advice. Try to focus on your present and let go of the worries that keep you awake at night about your children. They are going to do just fine and with mindfulness in practice, and make better decisions for themselves as they grow older. So, savor what you have today and cherish every moment you have with your toddler. Soon you are going to miss these tantrums and their constant need for you to tend to them.

Start Walking

Walking or brisk walking has a significant impact on our mind and body. For starters, it releases the happy endorphins in our system, which combat stress and worry. Then, it also serves as a means to energize your body and an excuse to enjoy the outdoors for a breath of fresh air. If you have a little one to take care of, how about putting them in a stroller and going for a little walk to the park?

Enjoy Some "Me" Time

We talked about this, as well, in relation to self-care. Doing something just for yourself so that you have the energy and positive attitude to tackle whatever life brings. It could mean lighting up some scented candles, having a glass of wine, and gifting yourself a relaxing bath to release all the negative thoughts and fatigue from your system. It is important to enjoy some time on your own so that you can use that to ponder over the things bothering you. You can also use that time to simply let go of any negative energies from your body by listening to guided meditations or songs that calm you down. The goal should be to unwind in that time of brief solitude and think about your personal goals and the means to achieve them. Indulge in self-motivating thoughts such as where would you like to see yourself ten years from now and visualize how good your life will be. You will instantly feel happiness settling in as that picture of you enjoying a vacation in the Bahamas comes to mind. You can also use that time to charge your batteries and before getting back to playing the role of a parent to your kid.

Interact More

Social connections are another important aspect of self-care. No matter how packed your schedules are, you have to make time for your partner, family, and friends. Not because they are important but because it is important for your mental health. Being a parent can be exhausting. Finding a little time to laugh and share stories with like-minded people can have a positive impact on your mood and psychological wellbeing. Parents, especially mothers, need this the most. Make sure to take out some time to spend with friends and family so that you can get your mind off anything that might be stressing you, and indulge in some carefree time with your pals and family.

Have a "Not To-do" Checklist

With endless thoughts running through your mind all day, checklists can sometimes be super helpful. Be it a recital your child has been preparing for all week or a doctor's appointment you can't miss, having a checklist eases things for both parents. First, they serve as reminders of important events, chores, and dates. Secondly, they also list when all those things need to be done. However, many parents try to squeeze too much into a single checklist, thinking they will be able to get them all done in a day. But here's the thing. No two days are the same when you are a parent to a little one. Who knows what's running in their little mischievous minds. Therefore, to not set yourself up for disappointment, have a checklist with limited chores for a day. Better yet, create a not-to-do list of all those items you don't have to do on your own and can easily be postponed or delegated. For instance, you don't have to go shopping for groceries with a child who doesn't like shopping. You can ask your partner to help out and pick some things up on their way home.

While you're at it, aim to single-task instead of multitasking. Your goal shouldn't be to get more things done but to get the most important things done, and done right. The idea is to stay organized.

Start Journaling

Creating a journal and saving your most precious memories is a great way to release the stress that comes with parenting at times. Some days, we are bound to feel like a failure as nothing goes as planned. For instance, we remember the time we went camping with the kids. Despite taking all the necessary precautions we could have imagined, one kid came back with an infection and the other with a cut on their foot. In those moments, we might feel like such a failure at parenting as these were the things we could have easily avoided. However, when we reflect on the event a few days later, we might feel like we were being too hard on ourselves, and there was very little we could have done to avoid all the camping mishaps. Besides, the kids had a great time and still cherish the moments.

Coming back to the original point, keeping a gratitude journal has been linked to improved sleep quality in adults. It also becomes a way to push out negative emotions because recalling all the good things in life is a guaranteed mood booster.

So make it a habit to keep a gratitude journal and write three things you are thankful for, each day before going to bed. These can be small things like a sweet interaction with one of your children, to big things like a supportive husband, loving kids, and a beautiful home. That way, you will worry less about the stuff that are out of your control and focus on all the good things you have.

What Are You Responsible For as the Parent?

This brings us to another important aspect of parenting; what role do you play as a parent. What are your responsibilities as a provider for your kids? Since we are bombarded with mixed messages daily on the "right" way of parenting, we must understand what our kids need us for and what are the things that they can take care of on our own. So, before you take advice from online strangers or relatives about the things that worked for them and what didn't, take a look at the role we think you have to play as a parent and stop comparing ourselves with others.

What Your Responsibilities Are...

Make Decisions that Seem Harsh

Yes, we said it! Did you know we think that we are not doing our jobs right as parents if our kids don't get angry with us at least once a day? It is your job to keep them safe, and if they don't understand it, then maybe you have to set some ground rules in practice. Of course, those aren't going to make your little one delighted but surely leave you with the comfort of knowing that they are safe and sound.

This also refers to stopping your children's attempts at misbehavior and letting them know that certain behaviors are not acceptable. They should know not to cross the line. If they are watching TV all day and not doing homework, it is your job to turn off the TV and get them to study. They may cry, scream, and whine, but don't let that melt your heart. Whatever you do, you do it to establish discipline and good habits in them.

Teach Independence

Independence doesn't mean you leave them to do the chores and lay on the sofa all day. As their parent, it is your job to train them to attempt child-appropriate skills so that they can refine these skills as they grow older. Kids who stay cocooned throughout their lives suffer from low self-esteem and poor confidence as they are so used to having things done for them. But if you won't let them play in the dirt, you can never expect them to learn anything on their own. They will grow up physically, but their mental and social skills won't. Therefore, make it a habit to teach them skills they should know to do on their own from an early age. That way, they will grow up to become independent, manage their own needs, and attain age-appropriate maturity in their lives.

Sleep training is a great example here. It involves training the child to soothe themselves back to sleep when they wake up in the middle of the night and cry for their parents. Parenting experts suggest that parents should start the training as early as six months so that the child learns to do it themselves. Similarly, at a certain age, your kids should know how to change into appropriate clothes, tie their laces, brush their teeth, and comb their hair, for example. You want to teach them basic life skills that get more advanced as the child gets older. That's the best way to ensure that you've raised your child to be a self-reliant, independent adult.

Set Consequences for Questionable Behavior

It is your responsibility to hold your child accountable for their actions and behaviors. This entails setting consequences for questionable behavior and setting certain limits so that they learn to behave well and abide by the rules set for them. They should, at all times, know that you are not a friend to them who will overlook their wrongdoings. They should know the house rules and that if they break the rules, there will be repercussions.

Accept Stuff as it Happens

There will be days when your little one does everything right, eats well, sleeps on time, and avoids misbehaving. But there will also be days when every little thing they do are opposite of what you wanted, giving you a tough time with eating, throwing tantrums over the sleep schedules, and get on your nerves all day. Those are the days when you don't have to lose your mind or blame yourself for being a bad parent. Instead of blaming and feeling guilty, find ways to cope with the challenges, and accept your child's negative mood and behavior. Your responsibility is to help them steadily navigate through their emotions, not lose your mind.

Pick Your Battles

Many times, parenting feels like being in the circus trying to perform a balancing act on the back of a horse running in circles. You feel lost and are constantly stressing out about whether the consequences of an action should be soft or harsh. This is the time when you need to evaluate which battles are worth fighting and pick them wisely. While doing so, keep in mind that you aren't striving to be the perfect parent, but rather a loving, effective parent.

There is no Shame in Seeking Advice

Finally, if you still feel that you lack the knowledge or resources you need to raise your kids in a healthy and stress-free environment, there is no shame in knocking at someone's door. We often sense the guilt and shame in the eyes of parents who come for help from us. They ask us to keep it confidential because if someone in their family friends found out, it will be embarrassing for them. True, parenting is something that deems to come naturally, but if someone you know is seeking some help, there is no need to shame or blame them. They are simply eager to know of better techniques to deal with child-related issues, and there is nothing wrong with that. It shows that they are truly concerned parents and want nothing but the best for their kids.

Now that we have gotten that all cleared up let's talk about some of the sources where you can receive sound advice and implement it with your kids.

Family: Your parents did a great job raising you, didn't they? If they did, then they are usually the first ones you can turn to when you need help. However, sometimes we don't want them to poke in our parenthood too much. Their views on parenting style may differ, as times are changing, and we want to raise kids differently. Despite that, they have still raised kids on their own and do have a few good tricks up their sleeves. Don't feel ashamed or embarrassed asking them for assistance and guidance whenever you feel like you are in dire need of some support with raising the kids.

Friends: Like family, friends can also be a great source of information and advice, especially if they have kids too. The reason they can be a great source of guidance is that they are easier to talk to and discuss things with because they have probably encountered similar issues with their kids too.

Teachers: In some ways, a good teacher can be an incredible source of information since they deal with dozens, maybe even hundreds of students every day. Many teachers have worked with hundreds, if not thousands of children throughout their career. You can bet they have some good ideas, and they also know your students in a different setting, so they might be able to give a unique perspective.

Online Parenting Groups and Forums: If you still feel reluctant to share your worries with someone that you know, there is always the option of turning to the internet for advice. If we just talk about a single platform, there are thousands of parenting groups and discussions that you can become a part of to stay in touch with all those people going through the same challenges with their kids. However, don't start trusting everything you read online blindly as some of the information might be wrong.

Parenting Resources: Since it is the age of the digital media, you can turn to many audio and online books on Amazon on parenting too. They, too, are aimed at making the process of parenting stress-free and enjoyable.

Parenting Support Groups: Like book clubs or addiction support groups, there are also many parenting support groups to help new parents ease into the transition from a spouse into a parent. Weekly discussions are held regarding child behavior, challenges with disabled and special-needs children, and how to keep one's emotions under control. You can also be an active member and voice your concerns and receive accurate advice from the experts. If you don't have the time to show up every week, you can simply join them when they hold workshops and seminars of your interests with parenting experts as facilitators.

Parent Counselors: Parent counselling is another viable and resourceful option when dealing with kids. Parenting counsellors help struggling parents understand where the issues are coming from to get to the root cause, and what steps must be taken to manage them. They are like mentors who have the knowledge and expertise required to raise good and disciplined kids.

Remember the saying, "It takes a village to raise a child"? Although we may not have the leverage to raise a kid in close-knitted family structures, we still have the power of more knowledge than ever before. There are many resources; between books, support networks, and your friends and family. Take that information with an open heart and mind. Sometimes it means you will have to go out of your comfort zone. So, don't be scared when you feel like you have hit a roadblock. Let your intuition guide you and give you the strength and means to tackle any problem at hand.

Be mindful of your actions and responses to critical situations so that you don't do something you'll regret later.

Chapter 5: Taking Ownership of Parenthood

There is hardly a moment when we are anything but a parent to our kids. They are solely dependent on us for every little thing. You are their primary provider. You change their clothes, make them take a bath, play with them, wipe their bottoms, clean up after them, and help them take a nap... The list goes on and on. New parents often see this role as rather permanent. They think that is how their life will be forever from now on. But the role changes with time.

True, taking care of a little child feels like you are all in until the end, but as the kids begin to grow older, their needs for you change. During the first two years, your child might need you for everything, but by the time they turn three or four, they require less assistance with things and want to to try things on their own. They may request to eat from a plate with a fork and spoon like their parents or want to be given a choice to choose what they want to wear. What seemed to be an eternal job begins to feel like a temporary one. By the time they turn eighteen, your children are less physically dependent on you and their needs for you may be more of emotional and social ones. For some parents, it is a hard pill to swallow as they are so used to being the primary caretaker. Transferring the reins into their children's hands can be difficult.

It's fascinating how, during our child's infancy, we keep complaining about wishing to have a glass of wine without being interrupted by the child for once or to be able to chat with our friends at a party without having to change diapers and run after our kids to ensure they stay safe. Then comes a day when we finally get that glass of wine in our hands and a bunch of people to talk to, but our mind remains focused on that little kid that ran away into the other room to play with the other kids their age. Yes, we as parents are quite complicated this way. When we don't have the freedom we want, we crave it, and when we finally begin to get it, we miss being wanted. Parent identities change with time, and it is a fact that kids need less of us as they are growing up.

This is what life with growing kids looks like.

Welcome to it!

The physical demands of kids change. They are mostly replaced by emotional ones. They change from simply cooking food for them to discussing issues with them, talking about their day at school, their friends, academics, and interests and likes. Kids develop an interest in things like sports, arts, and crafts, dancing, or playing instruments, and many of the discussions change, from what they should wear to what they want to wear to an annual event. Thankfully, there is little cleaning to do as the kids finally stop throwing food around or playing with it. It's bittersweet, but also great.

Parents, who we have worked with, report that as their children grow older, they have more free time for self-care and personal activities. They also mention increased productivity at work and improvement in overall mood as they have one less thing to worry about or invest their energy on. Many parents also state that they can juggle work and life better as the kids need less parental involvement in everything they do.

Our expectations as parents further evolve, as well. Many women, especially those who work, have shared with us that they feel more comfortable in taking on challenging projects since they now have the freedom to give their work the time it deserves.

When kids enter their teen years, the conversations and dynamics of the relationship once again change. However, it greatly depends on how much the kid trusts their parents. If they know that they will be judged and ridiculed when they come to you for advice, the relationship will be less than comfortable. Similarly, if they know that they won't be judged or ridiculed, the relationship will be more connected and stronger. The conversations change from friends to crushes and higher studies prospects. The interests change from building tree houses to full-time careers and apprenticeships.

In a nutshell, the role of a parent evolves with time, and it is solely on us to make the best of those changes. Keep in mind, as a parent, your foremost job is to be their mentor and friend so that you both are comfortable sharing ideas and talking about anything and everything. Mindful parenting plays a crucial role in that, and this is why we keep chanting the mantra over and over again.

How Mindfulness Helps Manage an Adolescent's Nuances

In a survey from the American Psychological Association, teenagers report the highest levels of stress than any other cohort of humans (Bethune, 2014). The uncertainty about the future and not having a defined identity leaves them in immense pressure, which usually goes unaddressed. The same research also reports that sixty per cent of teenagers don't know how to manage their stress. They mostly turn to the internet for comfort, and upon glancing at the "wonderful" lives of others, it leaves them further unmotivated and stressed.

Therefore, as their parent, it is your job to help them overcome the stressful emotions and learn to manage them from an early age. This is where mindfulness comes into play. Teaching about mindfulness from an early stage helps kids develop emotional-intelligence – the art of managing their emotions as they come and not let the negative ones overwhelm them. However, if you have missed out on the memo and have a child in his teenage years struggling to make it past every day due to existential crisis or a lack of direction, it is still not too late to start with mindfulness exercises.

Teens mostly see the world as black or white. They either think that something is achievable, or it isn't. They feel a wide range of strong emotions, like fascination, regrets, anger, and sadness, a majority of the time. Because their sense of self is still developing, they also prone to low self-esteem issues and poor confidence levels; things essential for their mental health. And the worst part, they are less expressive of complex emotions than they used to when they were kids. They sometimes prefer seclusion and being left alone to deal with things on their own. Many teens subscribe to what can be described as a fixed mindset, which suggests that a person is born with all their talents and skills, and can't really develop new skills, so there is no point in trying or making an effort. Instead, they should foster a growth mindset, and with mindfulness, you can help develop that in them.

Mindfulness teaches them to be more expressive and communicative. It doesn't promote suppressing or ignoring emotions. It makes their mind better at stepping back and processing things better and knowing how to respond to them more adeptly. Again, this takes us back to responding instead of reacting, which we talked about in an earlier chapter. Mindfulness is beneficial for teenagers who have trouble handling increased responsibilities at school, have high expectations from their family and peers, have gone through some emotional break-ups, or pose symptoms of mental health problems due to stressful social environments, arguments with parents or due to some mood disorders.

Below are some great tips for teaching your children mindfulness in a comfortable manner that doesn't seem too forceful, and urge them to adopt these habits for their benefit.

Why Do They Need It?

Being notorious rebels, your teenager will need evidence to decide on a course of action, and that is what you need to give them. You don't have to run after them talking about how great it is for them or how it is going to change their lives. Instead, hand them the resources so that if they feel like it, they give them a try themselves. Keep in mind that you can't make them follow something blindly because they need solid backing and reasoning. Lucky for you, the internet is filled with valuable insights, case studies, and research and implementation information regarding mindfulness. Gradually, introduce them to the many practices and motivate them to give them a try.

Let them know of the benefits that solely connect to them. For example, they are less likely to show interest if you quote benefits like soul enlightenment or self-actualization. However, they will be more intrigued if you put forward benefits like how it can help them perform better in their exams (Mrazek, Franklin, Phillips, Baird, & Schooler, 2013), how it can improve their concentration (Sanger & Dorjee, 2015) and how it can alleviate the stress and anxiety (Marchand, 2012) related to their studies. These are the kind of benefits that they resonate better with. Therefore, be strategic.

Model Mindfulness

Secondly, you have to lead by example yourself. You can't expect your kids to develop good habits when they don't see them in you. If you want them to practice mindfulness, you have to be their teacher. Model it yourself so that they don't have to look elsewhere. They will note the positive changes within you and take it up themselves. This is how you preach. This means that we have to handle stress efficiently without it letting affect us or the lives of others. It also means that we respond wisely and with reason in every situation, no matter how frustrating or agitating it seems. It also means that we stop judging others over their personal choices and accept the opinions of others without remorse or animosity.

Moreover, you can try to teach them via different exercises that involve more than one person, and demonstrate how life-changing it can be for them as well. If they are lucky enough to pick up on the benefits early on and begin to practice mindfulness, then they have a better chance of carrying on these practices in their adult life and being good parents for their own children. The point is to help them see mindfulness in action, and they also need to see that it isn't something complicated. When we sometimes talk about it with parents, they see it as something stressful and time-consuming. But if you have been reading the book and studying the various exercises and tips we have discussed, you would know how simple it is to practice mindfulness.

Teach Them About the Mind

To fully embrace mindfulness, they need to be made aware of how it works as well. Here's a suggested example to explain the concept of mindfulness to your children and how mindfulness affects the mind. Imagine your mind is like the mind of a monkey. Imagine it climbing from one branch onto another. That is how the mind moves from one thought to another. A lot of the stress we feel, whether it is due to our academics, relationships, or worries about our careers, most of it is in our heads only. Our mind is an improviser. It is designed to overthink and project possible conclusions. Without mental training, we have little control over it. So whenever we are stressed, it makes the problem appear bigger. Worrying further adds to our anxiety about things.

However, when we introduce mindfulness into the equation, it helps us see that most of the chatter in our heads is nothing but senseless chattering. We train our minds not to overthink and make scenarios worse. We stop worrying so much about the future as we learn to focus on the present. Mindfulness makes us aware of our thought process and gives us the leverage to practice control over it. This helps us determine which worries are worth stressing about and which are mere projections our mind has created. This way, we can manage our emotions and minimize the damage misdirected emotions can do if left unaddressed.

Owning Up to Parenthood

Your child is a child after all. They are sometimes going to be stubborn and belligerent. They will refuse logic, cry over small things, and plead in front of you to get what they want. You have two choices here – either you give in to their demands and be the likeable parent they want you to be or guide them into the behavior you want them to follow. Many parents opt for the former because it is so much easier and more comfortable, especially when we don't have an ounce of energy left in us.

When interviewing parents, a great number of them think that disciplining via punishment is the best way to instil obedience in kids. In some ways, this is correct; disciplining is indeed the right way, but how the disciplinary action is executed may vary. What some parents have gotten wrong is the definition of the term discipline. Discipline comes from a Latin word which, surprisingly, doesn't mean scolding or spanking. In fact, its literal meaning is "to teach." Disciplining involves showing them right from wrong. It means teaching them how to get over their mistakes and focus on the present. It means letting them know that every action has a good or bad consequence, and therefore, they should think and act wisely.

We have been introduced to an idealized version of parenting. We think that children are supposed to do exactly as told the minute we tell them too. They have no autonomy when it comes to making decisions on their own, and only their parents can decide the best for them. However, this is authoritarian and thus not feasible long-term. Kids who grow up in such households fail to develop a sense of individuality and often don't excel in school or careers. They usually have significant self-esteem issues and find it harder to connect with others and develop meaningful relationships. They lack autonomy until reaching a certain age in their lives. They also often act out irrationally and hesitate in taking orders and are prone to procrastinate and do the opposite of what they have been told. Rebellious, aren't they?

Toddlers cannot internalize hierarchy. They don't have the emotional maturity to regulate emotions and act maturely and sensibly. But that doesn't mean the disciplining in terms of verbal and physical abuse is the answer to their misbehavior. Instead of being strict, we should aim to set clear and well-defined guidelines to help pave their way to doing the right things.

Kids are known to act out for attention. They purposely test your limits by doing something naughty because they know that it is the quickest way to get your attention. Therefore, what we need are structures and preventive training. This means that we have to devote our time and energy into teaching them, with love and patience, and giving them our undivided attention whenever needed. This way, they will stop seeing us as authoritative, and more as a coach; they will gladly want structures and healthy boundaries, and they'll better learn how to be productive members of the family. They will come to know which behaviors are encouraged and rewarded and, therefore, must be adopted and which ones come with negative consequences and, therefore, must be avoided. It has to start with a laid-out structure in the form of schedules and routines which aren't rigid, but consistent enough that your children know what to anticipate and help them stay in line.

Discipline means leading by example and not by punishment or scolding. If only there was a single way to discipline kids, our lives would have been much easier. But since every child is unique in their ways, we have to adopt different ways that resonate with them. Preferably, it should begin by showing empathy, knowing their thought processes, and knowing how those thoughts turn into behaviors. Secondly, mindfulness also plays a crucial role, and so does emotional intelligence. We have to learn to criticize their behaviors and not them. We have to stop scaring them with the thoughts of punishment and educating them about ways to deal with their anger and frustration. At the end of the day, you don't want them to obey you out of fear or resent you for being so stern.

Take Ownership

Just because you love your kids dearly and are ready to give your life for them doesn't mean you let them run the show. They need to know who is in charge at all times. Parents who have a difficult time taking charge often report chaos in their homes with disobedient kids who have no respect for the words of anyone but their own. As their parent, you shouldn't give in to all their senseless and absurd demands, moods or whims. Many parents simply take the back seat because they don't know anything better to do. They feel like a captive spending life in a closed cell, waiting for their kids to grow up and leave.

But it doesn't have to be like this. You don't have to feel like a captive in your own house in front of the kids that you raised and looked after. You have to familiarize yourself with the concept of ownership, and own parenthood like a king or queen. Owning parenthood refers to taking complete charge and responsibility for who you are as a parent and how you are going to raise them. If you ever feel trapped against the whims and actions of your child, feel stuck in between love and discipline, then it is time you own your right as parents and be ready to take charge. Below is a brief description of what ownership of parenting looks like.

Take Ownership of Your Choices

We, as parents, make numerous decisions in a day. Some of them are good and others, not so much. But that is how we grow and learn. We are supposed to act all strict and disciplinary, or society calls us out for being vulnerable. This is the part where we try to hide behind the idea of perfectionism and call out others when they fail at something. But there is no point blaming the society, culture, or our upbringing when most of our circumstances is our own doing. We make our own choices when it comes to parenting. Sometimes we make the wrong choice. Some of us may have a hard time accepting our wrong decisions. Being parents, we have to stand up to the poor choices we made and accept the outcome with some compassion for ourselves. Owning up to our pitfalls and weaknesses is a sign of strength. It is the only way that we can learn to make better choices.

Take Ownership of Your Shortcomings

It can be quite painful to live up to the consequences of any wrong choices or decisions you made, but you have to own up to them. You have to face how those poor choices affected you and your kid and learn to be more aware and prepared in the future. You don't have to be too harsh on yourself as it is all a process of learning. When you humbly accept that you made a mistake that resulted in upsetting the family dynamic, you are being a parent and a great role model for your kids. There is no competition to be the best, and your kid isn't your enemy. Therefore, there shouldn't be any shame associating with learning from mistakes. Admit that what you did was wrong and that you could have done better. When your kid sees qualities like acceptance, letting go, and moving on rooted deep in you, they will strive for the same. When you admit your shortcomings, you allow yourself another chance to change your behavior and create a better future.

Chapter 6: The "Role Model:" Lessons Your Kid Can Teach You

Children aren't born with social skills or social knowledge, so they look up to us and imitate the actions and behaviors of the adults around them. Parents are the first teachers and role models children look up to for guidance and mentorship. Ever notice how accurately our kids pick up some of our habits (good and bad) like chewing food with their mouths open or sitting like their fathers? Where did they learn them from, if not from you? Kids are affected by what they see their parents do. They pick up on behaviors from us and often give us a clear reflection of who we are.

A child's dependency on their parents grows when they begin to make sense of their environments and pick up on our actions. This is the phase where we need to display ethical and moral behavior suitable for them to grow up with. This is also the time when we need to impart strong values such as not losing heart, trying their best, being honest, and being respectful, etc. We also need to prepare them to handle their emotional outbursts with calmness and counter any negative emotions using the presence of mind.

Kids view parents as people they admire, and they want to emulate us. Being their role model, we can inspire them to develop good qualities and habits, along with detailed instructions. Since a child spends the majority of their time with their parents, it is our job to ensure that whatever they are taught adds value to their lives and will help them in their future. These direct interactions are quite meaningful for both the parents and the kids, but can also be a little draining. After all, you have to be your best at all times. It can be hard to keep our chins held high and in full spirits even when we feel down and broken from the inside, at times.

The Stress That Comes With Being a Role Model

At times, the weight of being a parent is hard to carry. We have to be their caretaker, teacher, nurse, friend, and playmate on top of being their parent. Playing all these roles at once can take a toll on even the most experienced parent. We don't want them picking up bad habits, and neither do we want them to think that misbehaving is acceptable. We have the responsibility to preach wellness and improvise when we need to. Being a role model means there is little room for errors, as children are quick learners. Not to mention, the fear of getting something wrong can feel no less than a nightmare for new parents. The best way to deal with the everyday stress that comes with parenting is to become a mindful parent. Mindful parenting opens doors for improving behaviors and submitting to the things as they are happening. We have to accept things first to change them. Lack of acknowledgement can lead to poor decision-making because we react rather than respond.

During various surveys and interviews with children of all ages, we asked how they perceive a role model and whether they regarded their parents as one or not. Surprisingly, the majority of the kids held their parents with great respect and believed that they had a significant influence on their upbringing. We also had a couple of kids depicting symptoms of depression, poor self-esteem, and aggression. Upon some probing, we came to know that the children were modelling certain behaviors after their parents. When this happens, it becomes difficult for us to show them that they can have an identity of their own. It's a hard process but achievable, as we have to teach them to let go of those negative habits first, and later take up good ones. Therefore, as parents, you have to make the most of the time you have with your kids and try to teach them things that benefit them in building their identity.

Since everything seems too complicated, we get how stressed you feel. But you don't have to, especially if you want to instil good habits in them and teach them to adopt mindfulness. Why do we say that? It is because we have worked with many kids and come to the conclusion that kids are mindful by nature. They are curious little beings, love to stay in the present moment and savor everything that comes their way. What better definition of mindfulness is there than that?

Wait, what are we suggesting, you might ask? Hear us out. We are proposing to not view our children as kids but rather role models. Yes, the role has to be reversed. We are suggesting you turn into a student instead of the teacher and pick up all the natural and positive habits children are born with to learn a few things about mindfulness.

Can Our Kids Be Our Role Models?

Have you ever considered that when kids yearn for our attention and interrupt us while we're "doing something important," they aren't trying to distract you but rather bring you back into the present moment? They are forcing you to let go of your train of thought and experience what the now feels like. Since they are born with mindfulness, they can tap into that deep untarnished wisdom that we sometimes lack. When they call upon us to gain our attention, they simply want us to live what they are living and know how good it feels to be immersed in the present moment. They are a good example of how to live life to the fullest. They teach us things we have long forgotten, things that mattered. Take a look at some of the many things they teach us every day. These are habits and behaviors we can learn something from and adopt to enjoy life to the fullest as well.

A New Day is Here

A new day means new opportunities and new adventures. Even if the last one didn't go as planned or wasn't as exciting as promised, kids view the coming dawn as a unique chance to make it better. To them, tomorrow is like a fresh start, a clean slate and a blank canvas on which they can paint with whatever colors they like. They forget about the mistakes they made yesterday and focus on what lies ahead of them today. As adults, we should have the same energy within us. We should feel the same zest and zeal as they do upon waking up. We should see every day as a new opportunity to learn, explore, stumble, and then rise again.

Savor Each Moment to the Fullest

Ever noticed how sometimes children will stay engaged in one thing until they get it right? They aren't the ones to give up easily. They tend to soak in all the beauty around them and use their good time to notice even the most insignificant of things in their surroundings – things even we don't notice anymore. They will go out and gaze upon the sky and smile as if it is the first time they are looking at it. They will run after the butterflies and not stop until they have had a good view of it. They will take hours to finish the six peas on their plate because they have so much happening around that is way more interesting than those peas.

As parents, we often lose sight of the present and rush to get more done in little time. Everything we do is timed. We wake up at a certain time daily, head to the office to clock in at a certain time, then leave and return home, have dinner at a fixed time and then go to sleep at a predetermined time too. Everything in our lives can feel robotic, and we have made it that way. We have forgotten how to savor moments and live them as they are happening. If we think that doing more now will leave us with free time later, then let's pop this imaginary bubble of yours - right here, right now. Responsibilities will never leave you. There will always be something "more important" coming up, so why not focus on what we have today? At his moment?

Accept Things As They Come

Had the "worst day" of your life? Accept it. Didn't make it to the gym? Accept it. Didn't get your bill paid on time? Accept it. Had a fight with your spouse over something insignificant? Accept it. Kids don't judge. One minute they are trying to run away from us because we are feeding them the medications, and the next, they are coming to us crying because their throat hurts. It isn't like they suffer from short-term memory loss and forget what you just tried to do to them. It is just that they don't judge. They don't see you for your flaws or "perfection". They don't see an enemy in you. They simply see a parent – their caretaker.

This is surely something we can learn from them!

Don't Hide From Your Emotions

Oh, the noises that come out of our children when they are mad or angry at us. Oh, how wide their mouths gape open when they are crying at the top of their lungs because they can't fit into the door's little opening for the cat. Yes, they can be dramatic, but they aren't afraid of their emotions and don't try to hide from them. Kids are expressive, and they are comfortable in letting others know what emotions they are going through. They know that feelings are important and, therefore, they mustn't be bottled up. They aren't ashamed of their feelings and rather quite open about them.

We should aim to be like kids too. Instead of bottling up our emotions, express them for our own sake. After all, we have all had those days when we cried our eyes out and felt immensely better after the emotional release. Remember how calm and light we felt instantly? As adults, we can learn appropriate ways to express our emotions in a way that is healthy, physically and emotionally, for us and those around us.

Forgive and Forget

The same kid who was just disciplined for misbehaving comes to you asking for help about something. Strange, but quite common, too! It is because kids rarely hold grudges towards their parents. They know how to let go and forgive someone for the mistakes they made. Everything seems to mend alright with a hug and kiss on the cheeks. They don't allow a harsh scolding ruin their whole day or week. We should do the same. We shouldn't let our emotions get the best of us and hold grudges with someone forever. We should learn to let go too and not let anything negative affect us for an extended period of time.

Curiosity Keeps Them Alive

It is as if they live for the thrill of the unknown. Children are always running around, poking their tiny hands into everything, peeking out of the windows, and asking a hundred questions about anything and everything. Their inquisitiveness is something we should learn from, as well. We should ask questions about the world around us. Why are things the way they are? How can we make the world a better place? What's the name of that mountain range to the north of us? Why and how do ocean tides work? We should be excellent researchers and pay close attention to all that's happening around us. After all, there is a whole wide world out there just waiting to be discovered!

Conclusion

We have come to the end of this book, which was aimed at delivering the values mindfulness practices hold. We hope that this has been a comforting journey for you, and that you feel much better about your parenting choice and willingness to make the requisite changes where necessary.

As parents, becoming mindful isn't something only we have to aspire to, it is something that we need to cultivate in our kids as well. And this has to start right now because we all know the fast-paced media and advertisers are all against us by keeping our kids fully engaged and distracted. Teaching mindfulness to kids enables their middle prefrontal cortex to grow. It is that part of our brains that regulates the body, strengthens willpower, creates emotional stability, incites empathy, morality, and promotes harmonious communication. Aren't all these characteristics you would want to see your kid grow up with?

We can help our kids achieve all this and much more if we start to model mindfulness ourselves. They are going to eventually follow in our footsteps when they notice the positive changes it brings into our lives, behaviors, and moods. One of the biggest problems we face today is the lack of presence of mind. We have introduced several worries into our lives deliberately. There is so much we stress over and get frustrated about without even realizing that the things we are angry over are not even in our control.

Therefore, what we need is acceptance, something we have talked about repeatedly in this book. The practices we introduce to our clients help them become more resilient against negative emotions and not let them become overpowering. When parents embody the practices of mindfulness, their children notice it, too. There have been cases where parents came back to thank us for familiarizing them with mindfulness as it helped them navigate through their emotions better and create a balance between their work and life.

Mindfulness teaches us to respond rather than react, but it also presents us with many ways to accept and cope with the emotions we feel when stressed out or frustrated. This prevents us from losing our sh*t, which has been the goal of the book since the beginning.

So pick up on the habits of mindful parenting and start acting responsibly and rationally. Below is a quick recap of all the things we have covered, so that you can refer to things quickly when you need a review of some of the main concepts we've discussed.

In the first chapter, we started with what frustration is, where it comes from and why we need to take care of our negative feelings. Later, we talked about the changes in parenting today and how it differs from parenting in earlier times.

In the second chapter, we introduced you to what mindfulness is all about, why is there such a hype about it, and if it is something that is going to help resolve the issues and challenges of parenting that modern-day parents have to deal with daily. Delving into the subject deeper, we looked at how a beginner can incorporate some of the most basic habits of mindfulness in their lives.

In chapter three, we talked about who kids are and how they are different from adults. We discussed the various personality types there are, and characteristics of each, to help parents determine the identity of their kids and deal with their distinct needs accordingly. In the second half of the chapter, we introduced you to what mindful listening is, what role it plays, and how you can practice this mindfulness technique with your children. To help parents get started, we ended the chapter with a few specific exercises to try.

Chapter four included a discussion on self-care, and how important it is to take care of ourselves, so that we can be mindful and present for those around us, especially our kids. Later, we discussed the different roles of a parent and how you shouldn't feel ashamed to seek advice and support from the people around you. There are many resources, including books, online forums, meetings and private counseling, to help you become the best person, and the best parent you can be.

In chapter five, we talked about what ownership of parenting means and how parents can become more aware of what their role is. We also discussed how some parents try to fix things quickly rather than be intentional with their actions and change a child's perspective about something rather than just correcting them.

In the final chapter, we discussed what being a role model to our kids' means and what trials it brings along with it. Then we introduced a unique but valuable way of looking at our own children, and children in general, as role models. There's so much we can learn from our "kids being kids," living in the moment, and taking it easy on ourselves.

With all that laid out, we hope that this book serves its purpose and makes your life as a parent a whole lot easier. Before we leave, remember that your goal shouldn't be to become a perfect parent, but simply a good one with positive values, ethics, and morals. When you demonstrate these, your kids will pick them up too without you ever trying to implement them. Aiming for perfection will only frustrate you further, as there will always be times when your kid acts out, misbehaves or disobeys orders. It is up to you and how you handle that.

Take a breath. Take things one moment at a time, and, finally...don't lose your sh*t!

Help Others Discover Mindful

Parenting

Thank you for reading our book. We hope you enjoyed it as much as we enjoyed writing it. If you do enjoy this book and find it helpful in any ways, please consider leaving a review. Even just a few words will help others decide if the book is right for them.

We've made it super simple: just click the link below, and you'll travel to the Amazon review page for this book where you can leave your review.

Customer Reviews

There are no customer reviews yet.

More Ways to Practice Mindful

Parenting

If you haven't done so, here's a chance to redeem the ultimate mindful parenting guide.

This checklist includes:

- 3 Techniques to mindfully deal with difficult situations.
- 11 Powerful phrases for mindful parenting.
- 15 Self-care strategies that will change your parenthood.

Visit this link: https://tinyurl.com/mindfulchecklist

References

Beach, S. R. (2014, October 21). Teaching Mindfulness to Teenagers: 5 Ways to Get Started. Retrieved from https://www.huffpost.com/entry/teaching-mindfulness-to-teenagers_b_5696247

Bean, S. (n.d.). 10 Things Parents Are Responsible For. Retrieved from https://www.empoweringparents.com/article/parenting-responsibilities-10-things-you-are-and-arent-responsible-for-as-a-parent/

Bethune, S. (2014, February 11). Retrieved from https://www.apa.org/news/press/releases/2014/02/teen-stress

Ceder, J. (2017, October 6). Mindful Parenting: How to Respond Instead of React. Retrieved from https://www.gottman.com/blog/mindful-parenting-how-to-respond-instead-of-react/

Duncan, L. G., Greenberg, M. T., & Coatsworth, J. D. (2009). Pilot Study to Gauge Acceptability of a Mindfulness-Based, Family-Focused Preventive Intervention. The Journal of Primary Prevention, 605–618.

Greenberg, D., & Ladge, J. J. (2019, November 5). How Being a Working Parent Changes as Children Grow Up. Retrieved from https://hbr.org/2019/09/how-being-a-working-parent-changes-as-children-grow-up

Hanceroglu, L. (2017). Retrieved from https://scholars.wlu.ca/cgi/viewcontent.cgi?article=3069&context=etd

Jaret, P., Bullock, G., Kuyken, W., Hunter, J., Sofer, O. J., & Newman, K. M. (2014, October 8). What is Mindfulness? Retrieved from https://www.mindful.org/what-is-mindfulness/

Kallus, J. (n.d.). HOW TO BECOME A MINDFUL PARENT. Retrieved from https://www.gaiam.com/blogs/discover/how-to-become-a-mindful-parent

Killingsworth, M. A., & Gilbert, D. T. (2010). A Wandering Mind Is an Unhappy Mind. Science, 932.

Lee, S.-L. (2020, February 19). Myers-Briggs: What's Your Child's Personality Type? Retrieved from https://www.figur8.net/2007/09/19/myers-briggs-childs-personality/

Lindberg, S. (2017, November 27). How to be a calmer parent. Retrieved from https://www.headspace.com/blog/2017/06/18/how-to-be-a-calmer-parent/

Marchand, W. (2012). Depression and Bipolar Disorder: Your Guide to Recovery. Boulder: Bull Publishing Company.

Marschel, L. (2019, May 28). Emotions Discovery Bottles Inspired By Disney's Inside Out. From Laly Mom: https://lalymom.com/emotions-discovery-bottles-inspired-by-disneys-inside-out/

Mindful Parenting. (n.d.). Retrieved from https://www.skillsyouneed.com/parent/mindful-parenting.html

Mrazek, M. D., Franklin, M. S., Phillips, D. T., Baird, B., & Schooler, J. W. (2013). Mindfulness Training Improves Working Memory Capacity and GRE Performance While Reducing Mind Wandering. Psychological Science, 776–781.

Naumburg, C. (2013, January 27). What Is Mindful Parenting? Retrieved from https://www.huffpost.com/entry/mindful-parenting_b_2198097

Nichols, R. G., & Stevens, L. A. (1957, September). Listening to People. Harvard Business Review. Retrieved from https://hbr.org/1957/09/listening-to-people

O'Brian, M. (2019, August 28). What Is Mindfulness? (And What Does It Mean To You?) - Melli O'Brien. Retrieved from https://mrsmindfulness.com/what-is-mindfulness/

Rosas, L. (2017, December 22). Seeing The World Through The Eyes Of A Child. Retrieved from https://www.huffpost.com/entry/seeing-the-world-through-b_13784800

Sanger, K. L., & Dorjee, D. (2015). Mindfulness training for adolescents: A neurodevelopmental perspective on investigating modifications in attention and emotion regulation using event-related brain potentials. Cognitive, affective & behavioral neuroscience, 696–711.

What Is Mindful Listening (and Seven Activities for Successful Listening)? (2020, January 15). Retrieved from https://www.developgoodhabits.com/mindful-listening/

Williams, V. (2015, April 23). Once Your Little Kids Are Big, Your Identity As A Parent Has To Change. Retrieved from https://www.mommyish.com/being-a-parent-of-older-kids/

Printed in Great Britain
by Amazon